The Odds

The Odds

A Memoir

Margery Anderson

author**HOUSE**®

AuthorHouse™ LLC
1663 Liberty Drive
Bloomington, IN 47403
www.authorhouse.com
Phone: 1-800-839-8640

Published by AuthorHouse   12/17/2013

ISBN: 978-1-4918-4471-7 (sc)
ISBN: 978-1-4918-4470-0 (e)

Library of Congress Control Number: 2013922688

Thank you, Rosemary and Joyce, for your friendship, patient assistance, and interest in my Alaskan adventures.

1

In the grand cosmic game of life, the die was cast on a July morning in 1990. Two people from the extreme opposite ends of the U. S. stepped onto a small bus bound for Homer, Alaska, from Anchorage. One passenger was me, a 50-year-old divorced woman from urban Florida, traveling with a fellow schoolteacher. I was as forgettable as any other half of a pair of female tourists. The other was a 76-year-old altogether unforgettable man who had lived alone for 21 years in the wilderness of Alaska's Talkeetna Mountains. John Ireland was his name. We made unlikely candidates for friendship.

John sat quietly, not making boisterous overtures like one fellow passenger, a salmon fisherman from California who initiated introductions from everyone. My friend Rosemary and I thought for a while the Californian was our driver, so determined was he that everyone be part of a happy group. I should have known by his hat he wasn't an Alaskan. Alaskan men don't wear Adventure hats that snap on one side. The aggressively cheerful Mr. West Coast made a stab at jockeying to dominate the group. He rose from his front seat, turned and said, "The last time I was on Safari . . . ." There was a decided silence. The other passengers split into groups quickly. Two young Mexicans blinked, lay back, and went to sleep. They worked in a restaurant somewhere near Homer and were not along to see the scenery. The salmon-seeker settled for a "can you top this?" conversation with another fisherman and his son. That left John, my friend Rosemary, me, and a young man seeking camping advice.

The driver, when he finally arrived, obviously knew John and called out comments from time to time.

John wasn't especially tall and muscular. His long, wiry, white beard and well-used beaver hat set him apart from others. His eyes held the same northern blue as the sky, and when he spoke it became evident that he was estimable in intellect and spirit. There was a rather definite odor about the man. Obviously John did not frequent cosmetics counters, nor was he familiar with a wide variety of laundry detergents. What I thought was, "So this is a sourdough!" My guidebook had included Webster's definition of sourdough as "a prospector or settler in the western U.S., Canada, or Alaska, especially one living alone, so called from his using sourdough."

After the bus left Anchorage and was rolling through the sentinel-like spruce trees, John spoke unassumingly, without vanity or fanfare. His hands remained still; he emphasized his statements only with a nod of his head. "We might see moose along here." Seconds later a moose lifted her head, stared for a long moment at the bus, and strode away into the spruce. "A yearling cow," John declared.

The camper mentioned a reported attack by a grizzly. John advised him to keep his food supply locked away or high in a tree. "The bears that cause trouble with people are the ones who for one reason or another haven't spent the required time with the mother bear. They haven't learned the right foods to eat and the right ways to get it."

"Right about here we should be able to see Mt. Redoubt." He nodded to the right, and there it was. John knew the landscape.

Thus the day spun on. The camper and I were curious. In response to our questions, John talked of his 21 years in the wild Alaska interior, of fishing, hunting, guiding; of the leatherwork he did, the book he had written about his experiences, his opinions of current civilization. Of his outlook on humanity, he remarked, "I'd prefer Grizzly bears for neighbors; I know better how to deal with

them." John read a lot. Presently he recommended James Lovelock's
<u>The Ages of Gaia.</u> He said he had been to a wedding in Anchorage
and was on his way back home to Homer. How curious that even
though he had lived alone for years in the wilderness, he had been
invited to a wedding, of all things.

The bus stopped in Soldatna so we could have lunch. John went
off with the young camper. Rosemary and I went to another part
of the restaurant, where we discussed this interesting character
fate had placed in the bus seat in front of us. Rosemary was more
amused than intrigued, with me as well as John. She is cautious; I
am curious. But she is tactful. When she comes upon something
strange, many times she mutters, "Oh, my." She is too polite to
elaborate. Rosemary was married. She was always trying to pair me
up with Gene Hackman types. John was not even close to her idea
of a suitable companion. It was in no one's thoughts or imaginations
that I'd be in that same restaurant at 3 a.m. one year hence, seated
next to John at the counter. For the moment I just enjoyed my
sandwich and looked forward to more conversation with John on the
bus ride to Homer.

The day was the best kind of Alaska day: a combination of
warm sun, clear skies, and bracing air. Vistas stretched for miles
rather than being obscured by blue-gray Alaskan clouds. In my
memory it remains as a magic day—one of those infrequent,
treasured times when the world seems pristine and one is completely
contented. The world seemed full of possibilities. I did not know
then how many more days like this would be offered to me, or by
whom.

After lunch, John inquired as to our plans in Homer. He
mentioned some places we should visit: an overlook, the Homer Spit,
an antique shop, an artists' cooperative. When he learned we would
be on foot without access to a car, he offered to pick us up at our
motel and drive us to the overlook where we would be able to see
across Kachemak Bay to the surrounding volcanoes and mountains.
I immediately accepted for both of us. Rosemary jabbed me with her
elbow, looked at me with round eyes, and said, "Oh, my!"

The bus dropped Rosemary and me at our motel. John reminded us that he would be back at 7 p.m.

Alaska in the summer is perfect for touring, for darkness doesn't descend until nearly midnight. Rosemary and I tossed our bags in the room, noted that the motel had a washer and drier, and set off on foot. The day was still bright as a new penny. We made it to the Pratt Museum to see a display about the Valdez oil spill; enjoyed the wildflower garden outside.

Homer is a small town. Since Rosemary and I lived in an urban territory, we thought it prudent to ask a few ladies in the museum if they were acquainted with a man named John Ireland. We had been advised that the odds were good at meeting men in Alaska, after all. But supposedly, the goods were odd. The ladies smiled and said "Oh, yes! We know John. He's a wonderful person." Rosemary relaxed.

Our intention was to walk to the artists' cooperative after the museum. Halfway there, suddenly one step more seemed impossible. We staggered back to our room and fell into our beds for a short nap.

Seven o'clock came soon. John picked us up in his 1974 Dodge pick-up, of multi-colored body parts and what looked like a bullet hole in the windshield. Rosemary's eyes grew rounder and she whispered another "Oh, my." The hole *could* have been from a rock, after all.

We drove out of Homer to the west, upwards to the panorama he had promised. After a week and a half in Alaska I had run out of adjectives to describe the landscape and the sense of possibility of what one might see next. Alaska grabs a person and doesn't let go. Of a late summer's day, there is blue everywhere, in the water, in the sky, in the mountains and in the glacial snow on top of the mountains. The air seems pure; distilled. Pristine, endless vistas stretch out and up. Wildflowers are everywhere. A person can take a walk along the edge of a town and pick enough wild berries for a meal. Folks aren't surprised to see an eagle or a moose. I could only stand and look, filled with wordless energy.

I took a photograph of the bay. It's pretty enough, but it's only a slight representation of what it was like to be there, surrounded by vast amounts of air, with mountains and water all around, far in the distance. I remember I was shy about asking John if I could take his photograph, but he said he didn't mind. That photograph captured him well. In it, his expression is thoughtful; his right hand is curled around his binoculars (which he maintained should be called "a binocular"). His hand-sewn binocular case, lined with sheepskin, is dangling from his arm and you can just make out the hand-sewn leather binocular caps. He is wearing two jackets and several layers under them, something I learned you just do if you want to be comfortable in Alaska, making him appear heavier than his actual weight. His boots are hidden by tall weeds and herbs, all of which he identified and explained to us. The brim of his beaver hat lines up exactly with the horizon of Kachemak Bay, so there's deep blue beneath the hat and the lighter blue of the sky above. The evening sun, low in the sky, highlights the whiteness of his beard against all that blue. He stands as he liked best, alone before the landscape.

That is the John Ireland I met that day. The rest of the evening was spent driving out to Homer Spit, clogged with tourists, campers and fishermen. Passing The Salty Dog, a saloon recommended in our guide book, John thought "We better not go there." We ate at an upscale restaurant called the Porpoise Room where I was amazed to be "served" by a waitress with a New York accent, and a big city style—snobbish and rude. She seated us just where the sun sent horizontal rays into my eyes. John had his back to the window. "You'd better wear my hat," he said. I did. It felt an intimate gesture, but mostly, I suppose, practical.

Rosemary and I had made a definite plan to do laundry that evening, since everything we owned needed washing and the motel offered the first opportunity to accomplish this. We said more than once, "We have to get back." No machines were supposed to be used after 10 p.m. So John dropped us off. Instead of saying good-bye,

John put forth "I like to get letters." "I'll write to you!" I eagerly replied. Out came my worn journal. I found the page near the back where I had noted after reading and conversations, what to see in Homer: Pratt Museum, Ptarmigan Arts, Salty Dog, Porpoise Room. Beneath those, John scrawled his name and address. After 21 years in the wilderness, he had moved to Main Street in Homer. After a handshake, Rosy and I slammed the door to his pick-up and headed towards our laundry. John chugged off, and was gone. Later I wondered why, when this important link was being forged in my life, I was so concerned with laundry.

FORGET-ME-NOT

(Alaska State Flower)

2

So how did I come to be in Alaska at all? Through 14 years of little moments and big events. I grew up in Ohio, married young, got my teaching degree from Syracuse University, and followed my husband around the country as he took one engineering job after another for 13 years. Our son was born in 1967. Two more pregnancies ended in a miscarriage and a still birth. We did not survive the heartbreak despite our love and pride in our son. We divorced in 1973. After the divorce my ex-husband took my son back-packing in Alaska. When I heard his stories and saw his snapshots, the seed was planted. It was a long time before the seed took root, grew, and flowered.

I bought a house; turned it into a home for my son and me. After my doctor surprised me with a diagnosis of cancer, and successfully treated it, I knew I'd have to stop saying "One day I will . . ." and set some goals; be open to opportunities. My first goal was to travel to England. I was able to finance the trip by the sale of five of my pen and ink drawings. I had been exhibiting at sidewalk art shows to supplement my teaching salary. It was an expedition through family history, a revelation of love, a story in itself. My son and I walked the lanes my great-grandparents trod. We met many family members who previously had been only names.

Through my son's high school years, North Carolina became our second home of the heart. We spent a few weeks there every summer, with my mother, friends, and cousins. For me, it was lazy afternoons reading books on a shaded deck, driving through the mountains, drawing barns and wildflowers, and achieving some adventures climbing waterfalls. My life was happy and healthy, if not wealthy. I bought some land in the mountains, and my dream was to build a cabin on it.

My son took on high school with purpose. Guy, growing up in a broken home, an only child of a working mother, statistically could have become a juvenile delinquent. Instead, he became his class valedictorian and was accepted into Princeton.

An Air Force scholarship made it possible, but still, what money I had went to board and room, and the traveling I did was all northward to New Jersey. I visited him at least once a year, sometimes twice, to share a bit of his life with him there. It was heady stuff. Princeton's campus enthralled me: trees planted in George Washington's age, cannon scars on Nassau Hall, soaring spires, intricate gargoyles peering out from corners, dozens of archways ringing with collegiate singing groups, rich libraries, dorms with sitting rooms and fireplaces, intellectual action everywhere, wry humor in the half-time shows at football games; interesting people. Ask me what proud means. It filled me time and again, but overwhelmed me during graduation week when the announcement was made that his degree would be *cum laude*.

Of course my son then owed some years of his life to the Air Force, so he was off on his own, financially independent in whatever corner of the world he was sent. Coincidentally, I had more funds to dispense on possible adventures.

I had some relationships with men during all those years, some more interesting than others, none with staying power. On balance, there was an equal amount of tears and laughter. Just as before our trip to England, an awful experience brought to fruition my trip to Alaska.

The man of my hopes came into my life. He liked me. I never waited a moment wondering if he'd call. We liked the same music, movies, food, activities; we were close to the same age, both divorced. I'd tell him how happy he made me, and he'd reply, "You're supposed to be happy." My mother liked him, my friends liked him, and he liked all of them. He could build or fix anything. I could see a cabin going up on that land in North Carolina.

Three months after we met, he was diagnosed with pancreatic cancer. He died before the year was over. I had to have another dream. Alaska became the dream.

I began looking for someone to go with me. All my friends knew my goal; most of them were uninterested or unwilling to spend the necessary money. Rosemary, one evening before our aerobics class, said, "I'll go with you. My husband has been there twice. He doesn't want to go again, but wants me to see it." We began our plan.

Did we plan! There were to be no cruises for us, or any fancy clothes. Our travel agent investigated everything for us—trains, ferries, places accessible by walking, rafting, hops on small planes and boats. Guy, too, was full of advice of where to go and what to do. Six months later, we were in Alaska, and halfway through the three weeks of our trip, we climbed on that bus bound for Homer.

John's journey through life toward our meeting surely must have been as winding as mine, though he did not talk much about it. He told me his mother died when he was very young, and that an aunt had reared him. He had learned leather craft in the Cavalry. It took many years to learn a little more about his early life, but he never did fully explain his choice to live alone in Alaska. He talked a lot about many things: land, animals, flowers, herbs, fishing, flying, crafts, books, but not about himself.

Rosemary and I took a ferry out of Homer the next day, and visited Kodiak Island, where we watched eagles hunting from the blue sky and otters playing in the blue beneath. We continued on by ferry to Seward, where we caught a self-propelled one car diesel train back to Anchorage. *Really* no more adjectives left by now.

What a ride! We flew into Juneau and spent some time in Glacier Bay. I was keenly aware of each day's passing, less and less time to spend in the giant beauty of Alaska.

Suddenly we were home again. Rosemary settled into her married life, and I got out my paper and pen. I wrote a rather formal letter:

"Thank you for showing Rosemary and me around Homer. It was kind of you to take the time to be friendly to two strangers. It was a particular pleasure for me to meet you and listen to your stories. I'd consider it an honor if you'd correspond with me and tell me more about your life. In return I could offer you some stories about my experiences, though they're less bold adventures than yours. Alaska worked its magic on me. I was sad to leave."

I did wonder if he'd write. It seemed strange to me, and still does, that a man who chose to live alone in the wilderness for more than 21 years was so outgoing and interested in meeting strangers. But write he did, on August 2.

"Y'r card/note rec., gratefully—I hoped you would. Unlike you, I handwrite badly, so all correspondence is typed—using 'two index fingers on this ancient Underwood, by "Hunt and Peck" method. I've had this Typer ca. 37 years. Bought Surplus for $15; now it's considered "Antique." . . . *Perhaps we struck a mutual "spark;" I liked your style, quick sense of humor;* (one year later, he told me I had reminded him of the lady who had reared him after his mother's death). *"Ordinarily I don't seek female company . . ."* (That turned out to be quite untrue, but more of that later.) *As for 'experiences,' I've written this book, now at my cousin's at Sequim, Wash—she's supposed to be trying to get it Published. I have only the one copy here, which I wouldn't want to risk losing in mail. But if when I'd get the finished copy, I'd send you one. I didn't write it to make money, rather to pay back the wilderness environment for its support of me during more than two decades . . . it never let me down. It was like: I was careful for It and It seemed grateful.*

My goal was to try to influence a more caring attitude towards the wilderness and it's creatures in readers."

Then, the abrupt ending, which I came to learn was usual: *"End of sheet, I see; end of letter. Write again, please. Best, J. I."*

His style of writing seemed to emerge from a different century: random words capitalized, ca. (circa) used frequently, and droll contractions of 'll for "it will," and 'd for "would. Like writers of previous centuries, he used every bit of space on the paper. Using his Underwood, he single-spaced an 8 1/2 x 11 page, on both sides. I couldn't imagine where he found ribbons for the typewriter, but periodically, as our correspondence continued, the print was blacker.

John was as faithful a correspondent as I've had, before or since our meeting. He wrote about his life in Homer as well as his 21 years in the wilderness. *"I don't want a 'place' any more. With me it's either far remote, miles off-road, or an apartment right in town."*

"I walked to the (Homer) Post Office early AM, before 'd get crowded; I was the only customer upon arrival. I don't like waiting in line. If I'm doing nothing constructive, I'd at least rather be moving. But I've sat on a knoll with a binocular for hours watching for game; and sometimes it paid off. There's pretty country to look at, and always the chance something may show up from being hidden behind a rise of terrain. And sometimes 'd be blueberries or cranberries to munch. I used to think my year wasn't complete unless I watched a bull moose swaying his broad antlers around as he moved."

He wrote of crafting leather items for folks: binocular and camera cases, holsters, boxes and purses. Another task that kept him busy was saw sharpening, which he called, accurately, saw filing, since he did it by hand. He repaired guns. He took pride in doing careful work, and people sought him out. He was also a volunteer at the Center for Alaskan Coastal Studies, and at a local long-term care facility. I learned a few letters into our correspondence that he once had been a big-game guide, was an accurate shooter (archery and guns), and an expert at fly-casting. We didn't have much in common, except our appreciation of the natural world. I wrote little about my teaching, but focused on my canoe paddling excursions, fishing in the Everglades, and hiking and berry picking in North Carolina. He seemed to like it when I asked him a lot of questions. *"Seems you like hearing from me, as you include queries-requiring replies. Fine with me. I think you're a very nice lady."* Fortunately for me, he wanted to teach about Alaska, and I wanted to learn.

In August, I asked him to describe the weather in Homer. This is what he replied. *"Summer is on the wane. 'was 46F early this AM in town, 38 out East Road ca. 5 miles, made frost in Fritz Creek Canyon, 9 miles out East, where cold air 'slides' down to lower elevation in the canyon, during night. We're losing Daylight at rate of ca. 5 min/day, 'this Latitude/Season; still get ca. 17 hours possible Sun exposure, but noticeably less than Summer Solstice, now more than 2 months past. During shortest days, Dec.-Jan., 'll be daylight only ca. 8 hours. The Seasons show similarity to Tides: slow changes near highs and lows, picking up speed toward mid-times."* This was lovely to read while I was melting in 90 degree heat in Florida.

My life continued, as a schoolteacher's life does. He told me about the book he wrote. It related experiences with moose, foxes, gray jays, chickadees, swans, and beavers. It presented *"an understandable voice for the wilderness environment and its creatures, which graciously hosted the human (John) for as long as the latter wished to stay."* He said, *"If 'this' work should influence some readers to view the wilderness and its creatures with somewhat more consideration, a somewhat more gentle attitude, that would be all the recognition (the author) desired."*

The illustrations were by John, as well. He must have had a wonderful feeling for depicting animals, especially the large mammals. He had a thorough knowledge of the muscles and bones of moose, because he was a former big game hunting guide, and was also a qualified field butcher. When a hunter bagged a moose, John could cut it on site and pack it out. He did not kill animals or fish not meant for eating. One moose provided him enough meat for one Alaskan winter in the wilderness. If he caught one fish, he stopped angling, and intended to eat it. No catch and release for him. It was clear, from his letters and his book, that he had become a part of the environment, not a master of it, and wished others to do the same. He became an inspiration to me.

John admitted that he missed being in his cabin in the wilderness. He said fishing was too much of "a production" from Homer. *"Driving many miles, chartering a boat, all involving large expense, then mingling with a crowd of other people. When at the cabin, I'd just take the canoe, or sometimes walk if wind 'd make canoeing troublesome, a few hundred yards and begin fishing. Places I could go I'd have all to myself. And I enjoyed it: miles from anyone, crystal water, large succulent fish, sometimes a Moose or Caribou, and keep an eye out for a possible Grizzly. I'd have my rifle along—but never needed to use it for defense, during 21 ½ years. One comes to Make Allowance, for such as Bears. I'd prefer to travel downwind; bears smell one coming, get out of the way. Surprise encounters are most dangerous."*

I could only respond by describing my day trips of canoeing on Florida rivers, and my letters to Congress opposing drilling in the Arctic National Refuge. It was ironic to me that John, the ultimate environmentalist, was surviving, partially, on an allowance that all Alaska residents receive from big oil companies. I diplomatically refrained from ever mentioning it. This was one of the contradictions in character that, over years, was revealed to me. The other was his statement that he rarely "sought female company." In more than one of his letters to me, he described meetings with women who enjoyed his company and needed his help with one thing or another. One woman, he "could've married." More often, he talked of male friends who shared his interests in target shooting and archery. He seemed to be quite sociable for someone who lived alone in the wilderness for so long. He felt useful helping others, making repairs, shoveling snow, helping with gardening (which he didn't like much), and socializing with friends who would go trapshooting with him, or go to an archery range with him. He listened to the radio some. Once in a while he would mention that he heard something interesting, usually reflecting a rather conservative viewpoint. I remember once he said the Baptist Church wasn't fundamental enough for him. This put me off a bit, since I call myself an agnostic. We did share a deep mistrust of organized religion, however. He did read the Bible, and wrote, ". . . *hey, don't admire me; rather admire what God has done to make me— something He can use.*" I wasn't about to alienate John by starting up letters about religious differences, so I let that slide right by me. I did admire him—his wide range of abilities that enabled him to live independently in a harsh climate. Talk about self-sufficiency!

About this time I was becoming an enthusiastic birder. I had joined Audubon in order to take advantage of their canoeing outings, and during those trips I learned a fascination with birds, particularly as they migrated south to my area every winter. My backyard, planted with native trees and shrubs, began to provide food for my winged visitors. The first winter Painted Buntings showed up, I was thrilled, and wrote to John about the sighting. I should have known he was once "quite a sharp bird-watcher." He admitted, though, that "dimming vision" had "largely removed that ability." Weakened hearing had also affected him. I remembered when Rosemary and I had met him, he had a hearing aid in each ear. He went on to say, *"When living at my place in Talkeetna Mts. I saw Arctic Three-toed Woodpeckers from time to time, sometimes at distances of only a few feet."* When Rosemary and I were at Glacier Bay, on a ranger-led walk there, the ranger led us past a group standing in awe of a bird rather low in a spruce. Motioning us to be quiet, the guide whispered, "Three-Toed Woodpecker! I've been looking all summer for this bird!" That was in 1990. I've only seen one more since then, in Canada. To think that John lived all those years beside such a variety of wildlife was just fascinating to me. This was a correspondent I was going to keep.

Then in May, after we had written regularly for nine months, came this: *"I'd like to see you again. If you made it here, we could go to my former home in Talkeetna Mts., spend a week or so. There, you could actually get your feet on . . . Alaska. We could canoe, catch thrilling Fish, see really huge Moose, Caribou, perhaps a Grizzly. One would not go up there during July. It is a dull month, fishing poor, lots of Grizzlies come in after the King Salmon which run to spawn; early June or early August is good."*

My first reaction was: "Does he really mean this?" We spent maybe six or seven hours together before the correspondence began. Do I really know him? What would my mother think? How could I pass up a chance like this? What if . . . what if . . . I quickly wrote back that I'd like to see him again, too, but I asked if something should occur in the way of a health problem in the wilderness, would there be some form of communication available to get help? One piece of advice that was offered me was "imagine the worst thing that could happen, and go from there." I'm an optimistic person, however, and not one to say "no" to unusual opportunities. A trip to the true Alaska wilderness could be a National Geographic experience! And cheap!

Then in June, his letter *states "the situation at my former home in the mountains didn't look good again this year. Report by new owner there said 'was a great deal of snow, which would cause high water runoff, poor condition for fishing. In your letter of 5/15 you expressed concern, in case "something might happen to one," there. The nearest road is 60 Air (straight line) miles away. However, there is, now, a new-fangled radio-phone at a Lodge ca. 2 miles distant, on Stephan Lake, by which one could summon outside help.* (Did he really imagine that I could find this place, on foot, alone, if something should happen to him?) *Actually, while in the mountains, I felt more secure than around town; with my trusty rifle as constant companion, I felt confident being able to handle any situation 'might occur. And I never had to use it, as in a self-defense situation— during 21 ½ years."*

That seemed a mixed-message to me, so meantime I went on without making any decision about Alaska. The school term ended. I took a workshop necessary to renew my teaching certificate, and made plans for a different trip. A friend and I planned to meet in Atlanta; she would have her car there, and we would drive up to the

Carolinas and do some rafting and hiking. We were to be gone three weeks in July.

As the summer progressed, events conspired to change everything. First, the planned trip to the Carolinas fell through. It's strange I can't even recall why. I just remember that for some reason, my friend couldn't follow through. Second, another letter arrived from John: *"I'll write current owner of my former home to see if 'coast is clear' for us to go. 'D be Aug.3 or 10. The plan 'd be he'd fly us up to stay a week, then pick us up—he works during the week, has only weekends to fly his plane."* And within a week, another letter: *"He (the current owner of the wilderness property) sent thoughtful/kind reply Immediately (which I appreciate, as he's a very busy man) saying 'the coast is clear' and, he'd 'be happy' to fly us,' (which is an important consideration, since Chartering flight would cost ca. $300 from Talkeetna, 'nearest—besides ca. 100 extra miles driving each way, and ca. 3 times that leaving from Anchorage; (that's both ways, transportation, to go up, then be picked up), Besides having a friendly place to leave my motor vehicle. The way it goes: my friend/pilot works during week (Dentist), is usually available for flying only weekends. I have doubts he works Friday p.m. If we'd make the effort to go up, I'd think only worthwhile to stay a week, up one weekend, back the next . . ."* Then he followed with advice about planning my flights to allow for possible bad weather preventing a pick-up from the wilderness, and items that I would need to have, including hip boots, a good raincoat, and fishing license. He ended with *"So now I Pass the Buck back to you, and will wait to hear what kind of arrangements you are able to make."*

Talk about making quick decisions! What I remember is that my friends advised me *not* to go, I wondered where in the world I could buy hip boots in Fort Lauderdale, and that I lied to my mother and said I was thinking about going, but that John's friends in Alaska would be going with us. She told me later that she figured that wasn't true. My mother had stayed supportive through my marriage and divorce, and not once was judgmental. Once again, I pondered, "What is the worst that could happen?" Come to think of it, the cabin was located on *Murder Lake* (named after a native legend, I was told). What I knew about John from his letters was that he liked to teach skills and he liked to tell people about his life in the wild; he was much more religious than I; he was too old to be thinking of some weird sexual adventure; he had a fine reputation in Homer; he had a friend who was willing to fly him to his former cabin; and I had no real reason to say "no." My Carolina trip had fallen through; my personal life involved no commitments to any person or any dates, except the resumption of school mid-August; and after quick research, I knew I could afford the flight. "Yes," was my answer. I wrote back, telling him of my flight plans, my hotel choice in Anchorage, and said, *"I'll be in the room or lobby of the Anchorage Hotel from noon on, August 2, so you can find me there when* you *get to town."* Then I went shopping for hip boots, and I did find them. I also bought a journal with blank pages, suitable for narratives and sketches.

3

Journal: July 31: Anchorage, Alaska

"Marge's big adventure" began with wrenching departure (was I having second thoughts?) The book I had planned to read en route, Anne Tyler's <u>Earthly Possessions</u>, was finished shortly after the second flight left Detroit. Since my other book is in my checked bag, I was happy to learn that the in-flight movie was "Dances with Wolves." Watched it while eating lasagna and sipping Scotch. (Scotch was something I knew I'd have to forgo during my visit, due to remarks John had made in his letters. He drank only water; even disapproved of soda. I was going to have to be a good girl.) *It's 11:05 Florida time. Still sunny wherever we are—major river beneath us. Seatmate says Yukon Territory.*

I am alone.

Four a.m. Florida time—Psyched! Actually saw my bag deplaned as we waited for tunnel to be attached to plane, with some difficulty. Clouds hanging below mountains. Anchorage Hotel is great. Letter from John awaiting me with firm plans, reassuring. (Now I knew I had made the right decision.)

Journal—August 1—Anchorage, 52 degrees

Breakfast at Downtown Deli, reading newspaper found outside my door. Sourdough toast. Enough coffee to wire me for the day.

Heavy duty shopping, lots of walking, getting to know the city. Sydney Laurence (well-known Alaska artist) used to live in the Anchorage Hotel.

Every now and then the heavy cloud cover dropped to reveal the mountains. Rained off and on. My sit down at Elderberry Park turned out to be brief because of cold breeze and rain.

Bought fishing license and everything I had planned. Took very few pictures (this was way before a digital camera became my constant traveling companion). Actually got tired of looking at t-shirts and ivory carvings.

Lunch was Hagen-Daz and airplane snack left over from yesterday. Tramped around looking for place to eat fish for supper. Marx Bros. a bit steep. Finally I asked at hotel desk. Another long tramp to 4ᵗʰ and L to Legal Pizza, where I got Halibut. Food OK, but luckily enough, Thursday turned out to be Blue Grass Jammin' Night. Fun. Scruffy lot. Actually heard someone say "right on!" Real lost hippie type, skinny, wearing knit cap with feather hanging down beside his pony tail, one tooth missing in front, said, 'Music is such a neat language, not so much visual as auditory.' Like wow. Pity he speaks neither language proficiently.

Journal—August 2—Murder Lake—50's, rain

Awakened 100 years ago by noisy neighbors around 6 a.m. Went back to sleep. Up at 8:30. Decided on Phyllis' Café for breakfast, an inspired choice. Fresh baked scones with raspberry jam folded inside, and wonderful coffee. Rain. Walked to museum and saw a good exhibit. Some amazing examples of native skills of Siberian influence. Robes made of salmon skin, decorated with bird feathers and puffin beaks, which are shed yearly by puffins. A whole belt made of caribou incisors!

At 11:30, started strolling back to hotel, never thinking John would be there at 12. I bought an apple at the little grocery, and when coming across the street, saw a 1974 Dodge pick-up, fenders and doors not all the same color, and sure enough, John was there. He had just finished wiring on the muffler, which had fallen off on his way from Homer to Anchorage. His greeting was, "well, aren't you a brave person!" We gave each other a big hug. He came up to the room and I threw everything in my duffle bags. The hotel manager told me if we weren't able to fly out today, he'd save the room for me. All I had to do was phone.

We drove to Lee's house (the dentist) but he wasn't home, so we left to get groceries at Safeway. When we returned, he was getting his Cessna ready. I phoned the hotel and told them we were flying. Lee's house is huge—animal heads all over the place. All those eyes staring gave me a creepy feeling. He lives in a development in which most homeowners keep a float plane in the water behind their place.

Meeting Lee reassured me, despite the animal trophies. He was a regular guy, living in a city (granted, it was Anchorage), with a family and an occupation. He and John were quite cordial, and neither seemed to think it was terribly unusual that John and I were going to stay in the cabin for a week. I found out later that a cousin of John's had done the same a few years back.

We loaded up and took off. What a plane ride! Flew at 2600-3300 feet. We were level with some snow-capped mountains for a while. Cold, narrow rivers snaked beneath us. We actually flew through about six rainbows! Saw no wild life, though we all looked. And then, we landed on Murder Lake.

This is where I needed the hip boots (as well as for fishing and hiking. We exited the float plane straight into the water and pulled the plane up to the dock. The cabin, set back and nestled into tall spruce trees, was faintly visible from the dock.

There were kayakers and fishermen just leaving on another floatplane. The dentist told us he gave permission for folks to fish here. Some Natives, he told me, charged $300 to $400 for the same on their land. Land ownership must be tricky business in Alaska. I think, but I am not sure, when John settled here, he just found a location and built a cabin. He always said he really didn't believe in land "ownership," but in "prior use rights." But if that's the case, I don't know how he "sold" the property to Lee, or what happened to the people who used to live on his property. As I recall my adventures with John, I am constantly asking myself why I didn't ask more questions. Was I trying too hard to be polite and not nosy? There were so many missed opportunities! Many of them I don't realize until someone asks *me* a question!

He showed me a former garden where, while digging up potatoes, he had found an ancient ulu (round knife) and other artifacts. The fact that there were actual people here, miles from a road, reassured me a little. I figured if something nasty happened, I could go to the end of the dock and wave a plane down. Silly me. This was only one of two times during the week that I saw other people. After they left, a vast stillness enveloped us; unlike anything I had ever experienced anywhere.

John's cabin reminded me of the old mountain cabins I had seen in North Carolina and Tennessee. There were many outbuildings:

outhouse, meat cache, wood shed, storage shed for sleds, snowshoes, and a forge; and every scrap of stuff was put to use. The main cabin was truly a work of art. The logs were beautifully fit together. All windows were tight. There was a spring on the land, close to the lake. A canoe was pulled up on the rise near the dock. Outside was a "refrigerator." It was little more than a hole in the side of a hill containing a metal box. The hole was covered with sphagnum moss. We stored our cheese, sausage and butter there. When I reached inside, I could not believe how cold it was. Perma-frost is not far underground at that elevation. There was one can of Diet Pepsi in the "refrigerator, which John frowned at. The inside of the cabin was, well, basic, and, because the windows were so small, it was quite dark, even at midday. One room held a wood stove serving as a source of heat and a small flat space for cooking, a small table with two chairs, a counter with a basin, and scraps of leather, towels, nails, empty containers, a mouse trap, you name it, nothing was thrown away. On one peg, there hung something I couldn't identify. John informed me it was caribou sinew. "Good for sewing and making bow strings." Scraps of paper were posted around the walls bearing quotations:

It is unwise to sow seeds of anger; lest it flourish and spread, and bring sorrow to the innocent

Recreation should not wreck creation.—Paul Harvey

There were boxes of wood and newspapers. In that main room was John's bed. It was a log frame with a foam mattress on it, a bootjack underneath, and a peg for a hat on the wall beside it. Then I was shown "my room," to my relief (this had never been mentioned). It was a tiny room off the main room containing a bunk bed, lots of old pairs of jeans hanging from pegs, and one window giving a view of the outhouse. From the looks of it, Lee's sons had been using this room as their sleeping quarters when they were up there hunting and fishing. I stowed my belongings on the bottom bunk and planned to sleep on the top bunk. There was a leather holster under my mattress. I showed it to John, and he said, "Oh, I made that for a gun that's no longer made—a Smith & Wesson 22/32, 6" barrel, target model. You can have it, if you want it." The leather had a shine to it that could have only come from long use. It's on my mantle today. (And I really HATE guns!)

I peeled potatoes with my buck knife; John fried up the potatoes, an onion, then added two eggs. That with a piece of sourdough bread made our supper. Tasty. We ate at the small table, which sat beside a window, and looked out at the lake and the Sitka spruce that surrounded the cabin. Of course, it was still quite light. The light lingers until nearly 11 p.m. in August. So . . . . after supper, we started off to visit John's neighbor, Tom. "Neighbor" means something entirely different in the wild than it does in Fort Lauderdale.

Still wearing our hip boots, we walked down to the dock and put the canoe in the water. After canoeing across the lake, we walked a mushy, mucky, slippery trail to Tom's. I'm not sure how many miles we walked. It was a struggle for me, for the boots were a little large. All I could think of was Marlin Perkins from that old TV show, Wild Kingdom, saying, "We'll wait here while Jim goes on ahead." We had to wade across a creek. King salmon were jumping all over the place. John didn't like them because they scare the rainbow trout away from their eggs and it makes for poor trout fishing for the locals. While we were crossing, a moose crossed the other way! I stood there, open-mouthed, and John just said, "Oh, yes." When we saw an eagle in the spruce trees, John hardly blinked. I was thrilled to be back in Alaska; could not quite believe I was part of the wonderful land, for however short a time.

Tom's cabin was much the same as John's, but neater. It was hot and stuffy, because he had his stove going. He was also smoking Marlborough Lights and drinking vodka. John chewed tobacco, which he called "schmooze." This was a surprise—he had written quite a diatribe about disliking smokers. The men talked of hunting and fishing, and friends in common. I am still amazed that there was so much interaction between people who lived so far from one another, and who were so different in outlook. While we were visiting, the rain began in earnest. It poured. Then, the most beautiful rainbow appeared. It stayed in the sky the entire way back to John's cabin.

I will never forget it. It almost could have converted me to a belief in a deity. It was magical. On the way back to the canoe, a grizzly bear popped up to stare at us! John said, "Not a very big one."

When we arrived back at the cabin, we flossed our teeth together, which turned out to be the most intimate activity that ever occurred between us (not counting living in awe of nature), and for which I was very pleased. I knew then that everything was going to be OK. I visited the outhouse and climbed into my bunk. This is what I wrote: *"I am alone in the wilderness with a man I hardly know. There's a shrew in here. I'm freezing and writing this at 11 p.m. by the light coming through the window. I need another sleeping bag."*

Journal—August 3—38 degrees, Murder Lake, elevation, 2000'

Foggy this morning. Restless night. Too cold for me. Headache. Freezing when I got up. Slept with four layers of clothes on. BUT I'M NOT WHINING. Got up giggling. John said he slept great— always feels better up here. I remained silent and swallowed two aspirin without water. John said fog was a good sign, it'd be nice when the sun burned if off. He was right. Breakfast was oatmeal and raisins and sourdough bread and butter. Getting warmer.

John apparently followed a long-time routine, regardless of having a "guest." He repaired the stove pipe, cleared trails, and found many other odd jobs to do. He examined his former property. He had not been here for three years. I walked around, tried to help, held things for him, sketched a bit. It became a lovely morning. Silence was all around us. I felt small in the huge surroundings. As the fog lifted, the snow-topped mountains across the lake became visible. Underfoot, I saw, and John identified, Ground Dogwood, and Fireweed. The story goes that the Fireweed begins to blossom from the bottom of the stem, and when the top blossoms open, summer is over. There were only a few unopened blossoms on the Fireweed I saw. This is the same plant that is called Willow Herb in England. Similarities like this give me a sense of the oneness of the globe.

For lunch, we ate cheese, apple, and some rye tack. John set great store in rye tack. The shelf life must be years, making it a good wilderness staple. We also drank tea. Another product with good shelf life, and as warming and comforting in Alaska as it is to my English relatives.

After lunch, John gave me a lesson in fly casting, from the dock. Up, one o'clock, pause, cast. I could sense that fly casting was part sport, but also a good deal of skill and artistry. I had fished before, in Canada and in the Everglades, using rod and reel. Fly casting was a whole new challenge, one I was not sure I was up to doing properly.

John continued with his trail clearing and repairs. I wondered if he was happy with the way the new owners were caring for his former property. He said nothing.

I took the canoe and paddled around the lake. Me! In the wilderness! Alone in the canoe! I could hardly believe it was happening. The only sound was my paddle swooshing through the water. Huge dead salmon were floating in some places.

On my return, I questioned John about the salmon. Once again, John was ready to teach. He told me that after returning from salt water to the fresh water where they were born, they spawned and died. John said the best time to catch them is just as they get to the fresh water. Otherwise they get scruffy and rot. John didn't like to eat rainbow trout after they had eaten a lot of salmon roe. He said that they taste like salmon roe. He used flies that looked like minnows; then the trout that are still feeding on minnows will be caught. Naturally, he had tied some of his own flies. He used barbless hooks for a better sport.

After my idyllic paddle, we prepared to go fishing. John carried a "30 ought 6" rifle and a hand gun wherever we went. Where there are salmon, there are bears. He carried the guns in leather cases that he had made. We paddled a way, and then took a trail. I was wearing my hip boots with three pairs of socks and some insoles neighbor Tom had given me. The boots fit better, but it made for slow going through the muck. To my utter amazement, John located a walking stick he had hidden in the woods four years ago, to help him on the muddy path to his favorite fishing spot. Imagine! The trail had gigantic bear tracks on it. The forepaw tracks even showed claw prints. I took a picture of the tracks. John seemed unconcerned. I kept glancing around, but we never did see any grizzlies that day.

Down by the water, "the junction" is what John called it (the junction of Prairie Creek and East Fork), there were two couples fishing. They had just landed in a float plane (well, it was the week end). They were very friendly, and were smoking Marlborough Lights and drinking beer. The pilot, a fellow named Smitty, was glad to see John. There was much talk about flies, techniques, Native land laws, etc. All were taken with John, as everyone seemed to be. I was, too!

John caught a beautiful rainbow trout. The fish fought hard; jumped a couple of times. I made some casts, but had no bites, so when John hooked another, he let me land it, coaching me through the process. Then he released the fish, contrary to his anti-fish and release policy. This was his teaching moment, but he held to his other priority of keeping only what he planned to eat. He wrapped his big trout in grasses to keep it cool and damp, and to keep the slime from the canoe. Then he trimmed a small, Y-shaped willow branch to carry the fish. The current became so swift that it was difficult to wade. We sloshed back to the canoe.

On the paddle back to the cabin, we saw a beaver swimming. He saw us, smacked his tail, and dove. Then I spotted another, carrying a leaved branch back to a lodge. When he saw us, he dropped the branch, smacked his tail, and dove. John remarked that if the beavers were already working on their lodge, winter must be coming early.

The breeze freshened. Rain began to fall.

John, ever resourceful, had made a special tool for cleaning fish. He had taken a spatula and formed it into a triangle shape, sharpening all edges. He easily made fillets and left the guts for the gulls and gray jays. John called the jays "camp robbers." The birds made an efficient garbage removal team.

We went inside to cook. Once again, I was chief potato-peeler. I fried them and John fried the fish with oatmeal. One raw carrot and a cup of tea completed the meal. The meat of the fish was red and delicious. We had an orange for dessert. We chatted and did the dishes—a challenging job, necessitating one pan of heated water, another container to rinse, and both needing to be emptied outside afterwards. But no paper plates!

The rain began in earnest. I took a plastic cup with warm water in it, and a paper towel (Why didn't I bring my own towel?), to the outhouse for a very mini-mini bath. En route, I saw an arctic red squirrel climb to the roof. When I returned, John had a fire going, so with that, and another huge sleeping bag to use as a quilt, I had a toasty warm sleep.

Journal: August 4—50's—Cool, Rainy

Had a fire first thing this morning. Sausage, eggs, rye tack and butter, peppermint tea. I sketched the stove while John chatted. Who had he talked to, I wonder, when he was here alone? Walked around. Drizzling. Drew cabin from dock. and monkshood. We plan to visit Tom again.

After lunch, we set off on our excursion. We put on our hip boots. John gathered his rifle, handgun, the fishing rods, while I packed up my camera and binoculars. Both of us wore extra layers and topped them with raingear, as the weather was unsettled. Extremes in weather we had, indeed! Cool, sweating hot, cold, teeming rain, freezing breeze, warm air—all in one afternoon. We enjoyed a pleasant paddle across the lake. Then as we began the slog up toward Tom's, I began to get hotter and hotter. The ground was spongy with moss, the trail was narrow. Every once in a while, I'd feel rocks and tree roots under my boots. It's fairly miraculous I didn't turn my ankle. John was such a steady walker, and though he was 26 years older than I, it was hard for me to keep up. John looked for blueberries along the way, but didn't find any ripe enough to suit him. He picked mushrooms.

When he got tired of carrying the fishing rods, he hid them. I wondered again how he ever could find things he hid. We used the canoe paddles for walking sticks. What a walk/tromp/slog. What views! We saw a spruce goose, and lots of moose scat. In what I reckoned was about two miles, we got to a rise where we could see Tom's cabin. John said, "Well, I guess there's no point in going any farther. He's not home. His boat's gone." Oh, I thought. So we turned around and went back. At this point I really began to sweat.

John showed me an Indian mound. It was a dug out place with a rectangular "wall" around it.

When I was just about to give up and admit I was tired, John suggested we sit for a while on a log. Bliss. The mosquitoes were thick, but very few bit me, thanks to some good "bug juice" I had brought. Mosquitoes were one problem with which I had experience, having fished and camped in the Everglades.

After our rest, I stripped down to jeans and one short-sleeved t-shirt. In about 15 minutes, when we reached water, I was putting layers back on again. We decided to fish (Yes, he had found the rods again.) I began flailing around with the fly casting rig and trying to be cool and not stumble on the slippery rocks. John caught another beauty of a rainbow trout. He turned the fish upside down because he claimed that addled it and calmed it so he could take out the hook.

Then came pouring rain and arctic breezes. I was wearing John's beaver hat, which is a terrifically useful item in Alaska, especially when wearing glasses, as I do. No raindrops hit my lenses. I kept trying my casting skills, and yes! I caught a trout. Granted, it was a baby, but I hooked and landed it myself. John released it and we slip-slopped back to the canoe. We had a short paddle "home."

John cleaned fish while I peeled potatoes and cleaned *Boletus Scabera*, the mushroom John had picked as we walked. I must admit I waited for John to take the first bite of the mushroom to make sure he knew what he was talking about when he said it was safe to eat. Oh, me, of little faith. Once I noted that he did not writhe and drop over, I ate the whole delicious meal with a fire going in the Silby stove. There's a real satisfaction in living off the land.

I dashed to the outhouse between downpours, and then went to my bunk for sleep.

Journal—August 5—50's,

Rain has fallen, and the sky is overcast. The black spruce stand like silent sentinels all around. There are a few birds about. Grey Jays, I think. Another day begins in the wilderness . . .

When I visited the outhouse that morning, I found (too late) there was no toilet paper. This must be "wilderness man's" equivalent to leaving the toilet set up. Obviously John had been there just before me. A rather frantic search through my pockets produced a handkerchief, thank goodness. From that morning on, I carried some sort of paper in my pockets at all times. Men! When we were on a trail, John was always going off to "drain the radiator" or "water the lilies," and I soon learned all his euphemisms and did not follow him.

During our morning meal of oatmeal, raisins, and tea, we had an interesting discussion. John opined about religion and divorce. He said he believed what the Bible said, not what churches said. He said he felt a "strong leaning" to go to Homer and "confront the churches." At that point we ceased having a discussion, and I just listened. It didn't seem intelligent to argue about various translations of the Bible or the other contradictions that came to my mind in regard to rules of life. My eyes wandered to little quotations he had strung on a rope in his cabin. One in particular, said, "There is neither reward nor punishment in the realm of nature; only consequences." That didn't seem very Biblical to me. That seemed reasonable. So did the quote credited to Aldo Leopold: "A thing is right, if it tends to promote the beauty, stability, and perpetuity of the biotic community; it is wrong if it tends to be otherwise." But no matter. It was not the time for a religious debate.

He gave a very brief outline of his history: He was born in Ohio and grew up on Long Island. Somewhere in Connecticut, he had a half-brother. His mother died when he was one. An aunt helped rear him, and . . . I reminded him of that aunt. Fondly, I guess. That, apart from his having a cousin in Sequim, was all I got that morning.

Enough talk, I reckoned! John had chores to do. I went off for a walk.

The first thing I noticed was a group of gulls. They had been sitting in a spruce for a while, eyeing the place where John put out the fish guts last night. When I got down to the dock, the gulls flew away. Some camp robbers (gray jays) quickly moved in and ate greedily. The gulls screed as they flew. I knew that jays are aggressive, but I didn't think they would one-up gulls!

My next stop was the meat house, which proved to be the best, highest viewpoint for observing wildlife. What did I see in the water but . . . . a grizzly! I stood there, absolutely entranced (and safe, for there was a good deal of water between me and the bear). The bear was fishing in the swift current, at the exact same place where John and I had been casting the day before. The bear caught a salmon, and, rather daintily, began to eat it. The same gulls that were chased off by the jays were swimming nearby, picking up salmon scraps the bear dropped. How can an animal be afraid of a jay, but not a bear? I wondered. The sun shone down on this incredible scene; when the bear shook himself after eating, silvery water drops flew all around. And then he sauntered off, light on his feet, around the bend, and was gone. I had completely forgotten to raise my camera, but the scene is clearer in my mind after nearly 20 years, than any photograph.

My boots were wet from the soggy ground, so John and I spent the rest of the morning waiting for everything to dry. He was disappointed that he had not seen the bear. I don't know if he was sorry to have missed seeing it because it was beautiful or because he wanted to know what bear was wandering near his property.

After lunch, we prepared for an outing. John said, "It's best to let a fishing area rest for a day. Fishing will be better tomorrow."

We climbed into the canoe and paddled north to where John used to have his garden. It was no longer a garden; it was a beautiful hilly meadow covered with a profusion of wildflowers: monkshood, meadow rue, fireweed, wood anemone—lush with color. This is where John had found an obsidian arrowhead and an obsidian ulu. According to him, it was the site of old Native winter houses. How he knew this, I don't know. We sat and enjoyed the peace of the place.

After a while, we climbed into the canoe and paddled over to Lake Stephan, where there is a large hunting/fishing lodge, at that time unoccupied, but where boats were stored. As was frequently the case, I did not know what questions to ask. John offered the fact that he was formerly a field guide for visitors to the lodge. One time, he was told an "important party" was coming to the lodge to shoot a film. This "important party" wanted John to be part of the fly-fishing segment. The "important party" turned out to be John Denver. The lodge, to my amazement, had an enormous hot tub on the porch. It must have cost a fortune to put that in the wilderness.

From the lodge, we started slogging again to Tom's cabin.

Again, he wasn't there. Again, we turned around. It was a good tromp. I saw a caribou antler, chewed up by ants. I thought, "I don't care. I'll take it home." Then I tried to pick it up. It was so heavy! There was no way I could have even carried it to the cabin, never mind to Anchorage or Fort Lauderdale.

John found an eagle quill and gave it to me. I knew even then that there was a high fine for trying to transport an eagle feather out of Alaska, but for the time being, I kept it. We didn't harm an eagle, after all. I remembered visiting a museum in Kodiak, with Rosemary, and seeing a feather duster made of eagle feathers which the pioneer women had used to keep their quarters tidy. So I put it in my backpack. John also picked up some moose hair. He pointed out that the hair is hollow and provides good insulation. This, also, I kept. Couldn't help it—it was the schoolteacher and packrat in me. I still have it.

We had a "sit down" on "our logs" then on to the canoe. It was the same deal as the day before. I started peeling off layers of clothing as I walked, and by the time I got to the canoe, I was putting on my coat. Down at the lake, the wind was belting us from the South. Paddling through that wind was like paddling through molasses. We spotted another grizzly on the west shore—a real blond one. John said, "Not too big, but not too little, either." The bear gave us a good stare, and we gave him a good stare, before he disappeared into the spruces. John said, "Because the salmon are so late spawning this year, there are more bears than usual at this time of the year. This may have caused the moose and caribou to move a little higher." We had seen only one moose and no caribou at this time, even from the air.

Always teaching, John pointed out a plant called horsetails, good for scrubbing pots because they contain silica; crow berries, which were like dark, shiny blueberries; and cloudberries, which are apricot colored when ripe, and red, when not ripe. He was right about horsetails. On another day, I did use them to scrub a pot, and the results were satisfactory.

That evening, there was a fire going in the stove while we ate our meal of potato, bread, carrots, mushroom, and tea. John went out with his rifle to collect some caribou moss for me to draw. Caribou moss is lichen that looks like tiny caribou antlers.

That evening I wrote: *Low clouds, sunlight coming through, lights up the hills magically. Peace."* I recalled another of the quotes strung up around the small cabin: "Perhaps the most serious flaw in the human nature is the seeming inability to appreciate peace."

Journal, August 6—Cold, rainy on Murder Lake

Today dawned cloudy and unpromising. We had oatmeal, raisins, and tea for breakfast. We chatted: I finished the drawing of caribou moss while John went about his constant repair and maintenance jobs. Fire going.

Most summer mornings were like that in the wilderness. There was no need to rush because it remained light well into the night. The slow dawns and dusks were lovely, and so different to me. In Florida, night falls like a curtain. Light one minute, dark the next.

Around ten o'clock, I went out for my wildlife check, and saw a very wet grizzly climbing out of the water to the north. I rushed to get John, as he indicated he would have liked to see the one yesterday. By the time we returned, the bear was history.

I've tried to remember on subsequent trips, to do as my son suggested: When you see something grand, first, look at it, see it; then lift your camera, perhaps, or turn back to call another.

That wet, wet morning, John taught me to use a small branch to swish in front of me on a wet trail. That way the water goes on the trail, and not on clothing. It works fairly well on narrow trails. We walked a lot on game trails, and I was amazed at how narrow they were. A big moose, for example, does not use a wide trail at all. Their wide parts are well above the trail! This is one of the reasons they blend into the landscape so well and are difficult to see.

John usually planned an excursion after lunch, and that day was no different, regardless of the weather. On came the hip boots with three pair of socks, coat, and raincoat over jeans, t-shirt and wool shirt, and a hat to top it off. We gathered fishing poles in leather cases and backpacks (which John called sack-packs). John carried his rifle (taped at the end of the barrel for protection from rain) and 41 Magnum, and off we went in the canoe. It was frigid on the water; the sky was like steel.

We paddled past the beaver lodge, heading south toward "the junction." We walked, after securing the canoe, on a trail that was to me well-nigh incredible. There were caribou tracks in the mud, which John explained matter-of-factly. He went on to point out caribou scat, huge bear tracks, spruce broken over by bear, and grass matted down by animals. There I was, trying to watch the muddy, rutty, uneven trail without breaking an ankle and still take in all this information. A walking stick was a necessity, for both of us.

When we reached "the junction" we saw king and red salmon flopping and sloshing around. And suddenly, the rain stopped, the sun broke from behind the clouds, and the afternoon became glorious. John reckoned we should try fishing without crossing to the place we were two days ago, so he put down the rifle and we got out the rods. He told me where to fish and left me alone. I liked that about John. He never coddled me, didn't hold back branches—just expected me to do what I have to. I admit, it was stressful, trying to be successful at what to him were ordinary activities. But it was also empowering. I was living a life, albeit for a short time, that I had only read about.

I caught a baby rainbow (first!) and let it go. Then John caught a nice one. It was wonderful to watch him land the fish. Fly casting is truly artful—John's motions in those glittering, rushing waters surrounded by mountains, created a masterpiece.

Then John watched me cast a few times and gave me some advice. "Easy, easy, lift back to no more than one o'clock, pause, snap, not too low! Release the line, let the current take the line, point the rod toward the fly, and keep the rod tip high." Then! I had a fish! A big trout! John continued coaching. "Rod up! Rod up! Let it take the line but not the rod! Pull in line with your left hand! Rod up! Then, lead him to the rocks, slowly." I did it! John measured the trout at 20", and guessed its weight to be about four pounds. Whap! He struck it in the head with his small hammer, and there it lay in the rocks, shining in the sun and sparkling water.

Picture time! I asked John to take my picture with my camera.

He grumbled something about not knowing how to use a camera, but I encouraged him to just point and shoot. I stood rather unsteadily on the slippery rocks holding up the fish, wide smile frozen on my face, and just as John focused the lens, what do I see some yards behind him but a grizzly! Remembering that John had a hearing aid in each ear, I shouted, "John! John! There's a grizzly behind you!" "What?" I repeated my warning. John slowly turned around and said, "Oh, he's going down river." He turned back and took my picture. Then he casually waded to shore and picked up his rifle. I followed, doing my best not to slip on those rocks. We got our gear and started back on the trail to the canoe, me grinning all the way behind John, who was carrying my beautiful fish on a willow carrier.

I thought my outdoor lessons were completed for the day, but no. During the paddle back to the cabin, we saw signs erected by natives (and where were they, I wondered) saying "No Trespassing." John showed me small indentations in the terrain where natives used to sit, watch for game, and spear them.

Journal, same day:

We arrived back at the cabin. I stowed gear and John cleaned the fish. Some went into the "refrigerator;" the rest went into our bellies! John cut out the liver from the big fish and cooked it. It tasted like chicken liver. By the time we were eating, the gulls, jays, and herring gulls were taking turns dining on the entrails.

A bald eagle watched me from atop a black spruce as I made my way to the outhouse.

Back in the cabin, John and I flossed, brushed, and washed our hands and faces.

John said, "If you lived here, Marge, we could be friends. None of your habits irritate me." I could only smile at him, and think, "What kind of an idiot would irritate the only other human being in 60 square miles in the Talkeetna mountains, where grizzlies strolled by?"

Journal, August 7—Clear, 50's

It was lighter today at 7:30 than since we arrived. John declared it was a good day for a walk.

A walk? We started off at 10 a.m. and didn't return until 4 in the afternoon. But I didn't complain. That might have "irritated" him. I did spend a fair amount of time being amazed, for here was a man 20 some years my senior, who thought nothing of a tromp like we had. His first goal was finding blueberries—he called it "prospecting" for blueberries. (Turns out he had panned for gold when he was younger. He just mentioned that as an aside at one point.) He never found berries of suitable ripeness to please him, but I was eager to test them anyway, for I became very thirsty, and though we had packed a lunch (rye tack, cheese, and oranges), we had no water. I must have eaten a peck of berries, trying to quench my thirst. Unlike most modern folks, John was not in the habit of carrying water. He knew what to harvest as he went. That day John told me the best berries for quenching thirst were salmonberries. They weren't growing around Murder Lake, but later, when I did encounter them, they quickly became my favorite. They're a lovely salmon color, and wonderfully juicy. Alas, we had to make do with not-quite-ripe blueberries and the oranges (not too juicy, either) that day. I did think longingly of that lone Diet Pepsi we had noticed in the "refrigerator," but I didn't mention that, either. John definitely did not approve of soda.

We walked through the back country all day: slogged through swamps, thrashed through willow and birch brush, stumbled (well, I did) along narrow, root-crossed game trails and high-legged it through waist-tall grass. Up hill and down, spongy moss, granite rocks, cool breezes, hot marshes. My waistband and hat band were soaked with sweat. A few hours into the walk, John suggested we fold down our hip boots to cool off. Shortly after that, we had to pull them back up and put on raincoats. The mosquitoes were beastly in certain sections, mostly spruce stands and willow and birch brush.

John showed me the place where he once practiced shooting.

He remembered areas where he had shot moose and caribou, butchered them in the field and packed the meat back to his cabin. One moose a winter did him just fine, he said. Farther along our way, he pointed out places where he had chopped down dead wood and hauled it back to build his cabin. He said when he first built it, he spent the summer in a tent before completing the building. I couldn't imagine living in a tent even in the summer because of the cold and rain. The approaching winter must have been a good incentive to work steadily.

As we left his hunting grounds behind us, we found signs of wildlife. "See the marks on these spruce trees? That's where moose rattle their antlers against them." "These holes here are where a moose pawed the ground to urinate, hoping to attract a female." Then we came upon a lookout constructed of logs by settlers in the 30's. I wondered how he knew that, but, again, not wanting to "irritate," I asked not. Nor did I ask how he knew about a partially burned spruce tree that he declared had burned 150 years ago. John pulled a hank of grizzly hair off a bush. We came upon a moose antler. This one I did not even attempt to lift, but when John pointed at a moose bone (he knew the bones well from butchering game in the field), I decided that would do for a souvenir. I'm such a packrat. But I did use it later in the classroom for lessons about Alaska.

John called this "walk" the back way to Tom's cabin. There it was. And there Tom wasn't, again. This time John left a note. I'm not quite sure if (or how) he expected an answer. We sat on the steps, below the sign reading "This property protected by Smith and Wesson," surrounded by boxes which at one time had held vodka, and ate our lunch. I must admit, there were no cigarette butts about, even though I had witnessed Tom chain-smoking.

John went off to "drain the radiator" and I headed for Tom's outhouse. This was a truly remarkable construction. It wasn't the structure that was so outstanding, it was the depth of the hole beneath the seat! It was my guess that Tom didn't want to repeat the task over and over, so he made it good and deep the first time. I don't know how he even climbed out of that deep pit!

Time to walk "home!" It took us three more hours.

When we reached the cabin, I was parched and ravenous. I inhaled water and finished every scrap left over from lunch. What did John do? He immediately started to repair his "sack pack" to improve its bootstraps. Incredible man! I had enough energy to pick up a pencil and sketch. Imagine my surprise when John suggested we eat and then go for a paddle! Ever agreeable, I said "yes!"

The trout, potatoes, and mushrooms were delicious, as usual.

We washed up the dishes.

John informed me I was to be stern person. The paddler in the stern is the one who steers. This seemed to me to be a bestowal of responsibility, and in my weird way, I was honored, and also a tiny bit nervous, to be perfectly truthful. I know about how some men can transform once on a boat, be it a large yacht or a tiny kayak.

What a glorious paddle! John was a joy for a partner. Slow, steady, and patient. No effort to "take over." The only sound was our paddles passing through the water. The evening air was clear. Paddling south toward the junction, we spotted a young bull caribou in velvet. We looked and admired him for a long, quiet time. I steered us to the beaver lodge. Slap! Another beaver dove. I turned us around. We got a final look at the caribou, absolutely majestic as the sun, low in the sky, illuminated his rack.

There couldn't have been a better ending to a wonder-full day.

However, the day wasn't over for John. He immediately went to the spring for water and split kindling in preparation for the evening fire and the following day.

Water is key to living in the wilderness. Every day, at least twice a day, John would go down to the spring and bring water to the cabin. The water was clear and delicious to drink. We didn't need much for dishwashing, though obviously, disposable pans, dishes, and utensils were never used. Neither of us even mentioned a bath during the whole week.

Years afterward, at a dinner party, one guest asked everyone to name the utility each would least like to do without. Almost everyone, for this took place in Florida, named air conditioning. "No," said the questioner. She was born in Jamaica. "Water is most important," she said. We take water for granted. The questioner had been expected, as a young girl, to be responsible for the gathering of water. I asked her how she had learned to carry water containers on her head. She retorted, "If you spill any, you get into trouble!" How spoiled we all felt. It hit home to me a few years after that, when a hurricane rendered me without water service for two days. I've thought many times since then how few of us could be self-sustaining without modern conveniences. If we couldn't buy clothing, could we make it? Could we grow or find our own food? Could we entertain ourselves? Could we start a fire to warm ourselves?

Journal, August 8—

The week is over. John was up early today—6:30, and so was I. Solid fog. A good sign, according to John. He reckoned Lee would be here to pick us up, we just didn't know when. So we prepared.

John didn't want to leave without doing more repairs and organizing. I can't imagine what he thought as he went about his chores. Would he ever return? Would he die without seeing this place of such happiness again? Did he dread going back to "town?" I admit I had mixed feelings about leaving. Truly, I did desire a hot shower and shampoo, and a good laundry session. But . . . . how could I ever match Murder Lake to any other experience I might have?

John called me down to the lake to see a mother Merganser and her seven ducklings. Then I went to the meat house. The fog was thick and low over the clear water. Seeing no wildlife, I trucked back to the cabin for my camera. The view was magical when I returned. Slowly, slowly, the fog began to lift over the glass-like water. As the fog dissipated, it seemed a curtain had risen to expose an Alaska day in perfection. I asked John if I could go for a paddle while he worked. "Good idea," he replied. So off I went.

Paddling through the still water, I savored the huge, quiet surroundings, hearing only an occasional bird and the sound of my paddle: swish, swish. Alaska brings one a sense of possibilities, adventure, surprise, and humility, for so quickly, one can get lost in the vast landscape. I felt a link in the interconnectedness of life on the planet, and how vital it is to respect the wholeness.

I reached the beaver lodge and turned. Coming around a bend, I spotted a cow moose wading across the water, directly in front of the canoe. I froze. I stared. She went on her way not bothered by the canoe at all. She munched streaming grasses on her way, adding one more little sound to my ears. No need to pull out a camera. No photo could capture those grand moments, just as I feel no words can do so, either.

I returned to the cabin and prepared to depart, whenever Lee arrived. John knew it would be that day, but no particular time had been set. I was told to be ready in case we had to leave in a hurry.

We finished up eating our fish, cold, with rye tack, cheese, and water for lunch, then we set off on John's former "short hunt" trail behind the cabin. He searched for blueberries again, but there were no ripe ones yet. "Thought there would be," John lamented. "Look here," said John, "here are ptarmigan leavings. They sit in a circle." "And here, looks like a bear killed something here." We dug around in the dirt, and I pulled up a tooth. "A caribou incisor," John said.

Meadow rue and tundra rose bloomed on the uphill trek. This was the warmest day we had at Murder Lake. As John was pointing out this and that, I was happy that I could just walk it. He had not only walked it for years, but hunted, packed meat, carried it to his cabin, chopped wood and carried that to his cabin, and gathered blueberries and mushrooms.

Then back down the hill we went. We finished packing, in anticipation of Lee's arrival. We spent a lovely, lazy hour waiting for the plane. I sketched the shovel and sled that John had made (naturally). The shovel particularly intrigued me, for it was so obviously made for John's individual needs. At the top of the handle, he had added a horizontal handle, for better leverage. John questioned me about my plans to return to Florida. When I told him my return flight was five days hence, he reckoned that I could stay at his place until then (since I had no irritating habits). I agreed.

The lazy respite ended with the sound of a plane arriving.

Then it was all hurry, hurry. Lee had brought with him a propane heater and new stovepipes. Such modern conveniences! Caribou season was to begin shortly, and Lee was preparing for a comfortable hunting outpost. We were expected to load up our belongings and board quickly. We did. Murder Lake was soon behind us,

4

The flight back made it impossible to feel sadness. It was glorious! Lee took the long way back to Anchorage so he could scout game. All I could do was marvel at the mountains and rivers. I did see six moose and a black (maybe silver-tipped) grizzly bear. No wonder they're hard to spot. They mostly sit between spruces. One I saw wading across a lake. Then . . . we got the most magnificent look at Mount McKinley . . . all of it. It defies description. Mount Susitnu was also lovely. It looks like a woman lying down. The legend is that Susitnu is a sleeping woman waiting for her husband to return from war; waiting for peace. She's been waiting for a long, long time. A short time later, we landed at Lee's place.

John and I were hungry; no, starving. We got in John's pickup and took off. It was rather awkward planning the re-entry into non-wilderness. Although we had slept separately in two rooms in the wilderness, the unstated question was, what do we do now? Drive all night? Stay in a motel, with unknown sleeping quarters? First, we needed to eat. John stopped at a Dominos Pizza, but it was only a take-out place. The clerk kindly recommended a Pizza Hut, but we spotted a Chinese restaurant. "Oh," said John. "That would be OK." He did a u-turn and then drove past the entrance. We were on a six-lane divided highway. John *stopped* in the right-hand lane and *backed up* to get to the entrance, causing pickups and an oncoming *semi* to pass us! I thought, "Oh, no, I lived through the wilds to die on an Alaskan highway!" But we made it. John said, "Well, I'm just a country boy. I'm not used to all these complicated situations."

The restaurant was ornately decorated. Grating Oriental music was playing. The food, however, was good and plentiful. The waiter placed a water pitcher in front of us every other minute. And, to my humble gratitude, there was, of course, a flush toilet and running water pouring from the taps in the restroom. I had the opportunity to smell myself, and it wasn't nice. I briefly glanced in the mirror to see that my hair was a total horror. In the wilderness, these qualities were irrelevant.

We didn't leave the restaurant until nearly 10. After a few inconclusive comments, in a tactic to avoid uncomfortable arrangements, John decided to drive all night to get to Homer. No inns were open, actually. We stopped at Soldatna for something to drink. This was the very same restaurant the bus stopped at the previous year when Rosemary and I had just met John! I bravely ordered a Diet Pepsi, much to John's displeasure. He scowled and asked, "Do you drink that stuff often?" Ooops, I thought, as I answered, "No." Blatant lie. "I have no use for that at all," he replied. So much for none of my habits irritating him. I told myself not to make a similar mistake again, wilderness or not.

When we sat once more in the pickup, I totally expired, leaving it to the gods and goddesses that be, to protect our lives. We arrived in Homer shortly after 5 a.m., with relief and gratitude on my part.

John's apartment was quite neat and modern on the outside.

When we entered his quarters, though, I saw it didn't look significantly different from the inside of his log cabin in the Talkeetnas. There were boxes everywhere, as well as old newspapers, leather-crafting tools, mismatched chairs of dubious age. He had strung a thin rope across the living room, from which hung Christmas cards. Another rope stretched across the shower stall. He told me he washed his clothes in the bathtub and hung them on the rope to dry because he "didn't understand laundry machines." There was no telephone or television set, only a small radio-cassette player. His old Underwood typewriter balanced on a plank between boxes. In the kitchen, I noted an iron skillet with vice grips for a handle. The wastebasket was a giant Tide box. John acknowledged, "Interior decorating is not my forte."

I was invited to sleep in a sleeping bag on his living room floor, and I gladly accepted. He retreated to his room. I lay on the bag, fully clothed. The bag just fit between chairs and boxes. The pillow he had provided was covered with a khaki t-shirt secured with rubber bands. John disappeared into his room, and sleep took away any discomfort or amusement I might have felt.

Journal, August 9, Homer

Woke to the sound of mail being opened, about 10 a.m. Rose, showered (near bliss except for the towel); washed hair and shaved armpits and legs. Put on clean clothes!

How spoiled we become with small comforts. I resolved that if I ever returned to visit John, I would bring my own towel. His was old and thin, and didn't exactly smell fresh. In fact, it reeked of a kind of moldy smell. Live and learn. When I emerged from the bathroom, John remarked, "Your hair is all fluffy."

Now I began to know the "town" John . . . . exceeding different from the "wilderness" John.

First, we skipped breakfast in order to have lunch at the Homer Senior Center, where the price of the meal was $5. "Town" John liked bargains. Seniors in Alaska are treated with great respect and granted many good deals, not only at senior centers, but in grocery stores, which routinely have discount senior days. And of course every resident, man, woman, or child, gets an oil allowance just for living in Alaska.

The Senior Center was pleasant and warm. The lunch was about on a par with the school lunches that I routinely avoided, except for the tea that was offered: Stash Tea. I had never experienced Stash Tea before, and for months after returning home to Florida, I ordered it by mail. Remember, this was pre-coffee and tea bar time in Florida. During lunch, we chatted with a retired doctor and a former teacher, who gave me some tips on exchange teaching. What fun that would be, I thought, to teach in Alaska for a year! While I was chatting, John pocketed five or six packs of Melba Toast. Later, in his kitchen, I found an entire cupboard full of the stuff. This was the man who would not keep a fish unless he planned to eat it!

Besides the dining room, there was a room with pool tables, and quite a few men were shooting pool. There was a reading room, where, apparently, John was in the custom of reading the newspaper. He told me he liked to work the jumble, and proceeded to complete it without writing anything down. On the way out of the center we passed an empty craft room.

Characteristic #2 of the "town" John now came into play. We wandered around town, visiting all his friends. This—the man who lived alone for 20 some years! In Homer, he was well-known, well-liked, and more sociable than I! We stopped in at an antique shop. John displayed some of his leather work there. He had switched from making holsters and binocular covers to creating boxes, hair clips, and purses. The type of leather he used, though, was thoroughly military . . . tough, heavy duty, and stiff. It was beautifully done. The lady who ran the shop was a former teacher. Her husband was full of questions about what game we might have seen from the airplane. He was preparing for a hunting week end, hoping for a caribou, as was Lee. John was happy to give him advice and information.

Our next stop was the Mental Health Annex. I suspected that was a euphemistic name for alcohol/drug rehab. I met a friend of John's whom he had apparently been trying to help in some way. The fellow surely seemed to have problems. He didn't make eye contact with me or talk very much.

On we went to an art studio, where I met resident artist Toby Tyler. He had some lovely pieces. He greeted John warmly and let me look around. I resolved to buy something from him another day.

After the art studio we proceeded on to a long-term care center, where we listened (briefly) to two women sing accompanied by a ukulele. Men and women in wheelchairs nodded their heads and smiled rather vacantly. John said, "Let's go out in the garden. I have to check out what I planted." He checked out the vegetables and flowers. When he said, "I have to go water the lilies," I nearly followed him, until I remembered that was one of his euphemisms for having to urinate. John reverted to his woodsman self, even though there surely was a bathroom inside the facility.

Everywhere we went, even to the bank (I felt some cash would be useful). John was recognized and welcomed warmly.

John led me to yet another stop, where we made reservations for an all-day tour of The Center for Coastal Studies. John volunteered with that organization. The price of the tour was usually $49, but since I was with John, they said it was only $10. We were all set for the following day.

We had been gadding about all afternoon, but there was one more stop before dinner. John introduced me to his mechanic and his wife. John sought advice about that muffler I had seen him re-attaching in Anchorage. While John and his mechanic talked car talk and made an appointment for repair, I talked education talk with his wife, another former teacher. Everyone in town seemed very pleasant. It reminded me of living in Minnesota and what a great social life my husband and I had there. Perhaps people are more sociable in cold climates because they know one day they may have to depend on others through the harsh climate and all the collateral problems that may arise as a result.

It was time to eat again. Dinner was at "Family Dinning."

John said, "I don't know, it may be too noisy here for us." He didn't even crack a smile. Here again, people greeted John and looked at me curiously. John remarked that they probably had never seen him with a woman before. The mushroom cheeseburgers were good. We drank coffee. On the way back to John's place, he stopped to buy some New Zealand Steinlager at a grog shop. Upon reaching home, John fetched glasses. They proved to be Adams All Natural Peanut Butter jars, labels still on. The beer was good, and I felt quite mellow. Then, back to my sleeping bag and its t-shirt pillow case.

I lay there in amazement at the difference in the two "Johns."

However could he have lived in isolation for so many years and then become Mr. Man About Town? Did he have more visitors than I assumed in the cabin? Perhaps hunters and fishermen dropped by frequently. He did have one "neighbor," the elusive Tom. The "lodge" wasn't too far away from his cabin, but the people who went there used John as a field guide, not a social companion. No, it just didn't add up. John seemed an entirely different person in Homer. But, then, John didn't know the Fort Lauderdale Marge, either.

Journal, August 10, Homer—Overcast, temps in the 50's

Up early today—6:30—to prepare for the all day natural history tour with the Center for Alaskan Coastal Studies.

Before we left, John took it upon himself to shorten my binocular strap. He used his leather tools, and I photographed his hands as he worked. I love to draw hands, and I thought that would be a good project for me in Fort Lauderdale. Then—boom! It was time to leave.

We loaded up John's pickup and drove to Homer Spit. The Spit, on a summer day, is jammed with tourists and campers mostly there for the fishing. John called them "combat fishermen." Cars were parked everywhere, but we finally found a place near The Salty Dawg Saloon, the place John had recommended a year ago that Rosemary and I should "stay away from."

That day the tides were extreme—a difference of over 20 feet between high and low. The boat we were to board sat low in the water, so the ramp to get to it was close to vertical. It was like climbing down an extension ladder. Not an easy task in hip boots!

"Welcome aboard the Rainbow Connection!" we were told. The boat was a small version of an Alaskan ferry, complete with snack bar, bathroom, inside as well as outside seating. The crew, Beth and (another) John welcomed us warmly. The weather was not an issue today. Water was fairly flat, and though the sky was overcast, there was no rain. As we passed Gull Island Rookery, I spotted puffins, some of my all-time favorite birds. They are comical, so fat that even though flapping their wings energetically, they do not get very high over the water.

Tide pooling on Peterson Bay was our first activity. Because the tide was so low, many beautiful creatures were exposed. There were dozens of sea stars of different colors, sizes, and types, having from five to 24 legs. As we turned over rocks, slippery with kelp, we found urchins, worms, slugs, chitins, and hermit crabs. Our guides kept their eyes on the rapidly incoming tide, and signaled when it was time to leave. We retreated to the Center to meet another guide called Carmen, who was in the process of writing a book about her travels, not only in Alaska, but in Indonesia and Antarctica, too. She had a backpack covered with patches from the places she'd been. "What a great idea," I thought. "I'll do the same." Patches make a highly portable and inexpensive souvenir. On this very trip, I began my own collection.

(Years later my backpack was covered with patches from Alaska, England, Peru, Ecuador, Costa Rica, Panama, the Everglades and other parks in Florida. During one outing, my canoe overturned in the East River off Everglades City, and I lost that backpack, along with a cell phone and my car keys. It was the backpack I regretted losing the most, and I no longer collect patches.)

We learned at the Center that Alaskan citizens were working to buy back the land around the Center so that the Natives who owned it wouldn't agree with lumber companies to clear-cut the trees. We were asked to sign a petition. Alaskans are an interesting bunch. I expected more of the population to be ecologically minded. But as everybody knows now, the folks elected in Alaska are more often ready to sell this beautiful land to oil companies for drilling, and lumber companies for wood. Of course there is also the famous ex-governor who likes to shoot wolves from helicopters. OK, no more politics.

Carmen led us over to an aquarium. She told us to watch a sea star closely as it approached a cockle. We learned that a sea star, although it might be smaller than a cockle, could extend its stomach directly into the cockle shell and eat the animal. However, the cockle has a defense mechanism. According to Carmen, because of a chemical signal, the cockle senses that a sea star is near. It can shoot its foot quickly to push itself away from the sea star. We saw it push itself right out of the water.

John and I ate the lunch we had brought: rice cakes, cheese, pecans, and an apple. Then everybody took off on the trails.

"Whew," I thought. "I thought my strenuous hikes were already accomplished!" The trail was wide with few branches overhanging, but it was so steep that in one section ropes had been installed so that hikers could cling to them going up the hill. The edges of the trail were too close to cliffs for me. Many thoughts of Peter Matthiessen's "Zen of hiking" went through my mind. Unfortunately, I was not able to reach that zone, even after four and a half hours of hiking. Once again, hip boots were not making steps any easier. Neither did they make it easier to jump over a crack in the ground left by an earthquake, at Earthquake Point!

The plant life was diverse and beautiful: Devil's Club, Watermelon Berry, Monkshood, Foam Flower, Shy Maiden. The Watermelon Berry reminded me of Solomon's seal that I had seen in North Carolina; Foam Flower looked to me like Baby's Breath; and Shy Maiden resembled Wintergreen. I knew that Fireweed, which I had seen in Alaska the previous year, was called Willow Herb in England. Different places, different names, same plants. John was John at Murder Lake and Homer; same name; but what a different fellow! Same with me! Fort Lauderdale teacher and Alaska adventurer!

The long hike was over. We climbed onto a float which was released by rope out to another floating dock where the Rainbow Connection was to pick us up. The tide was increasing rapidly. The area where we had been tide pooling was now completely under water, as was the huge rock nearby.

After boarding Rainbow Connection, we passed Gull Island, where we saw puffins, cormorants, kittiwakes, glaucous-winged gulls, and murres. The excellent captain maneuvered the boat for outstanding looks at all these species. Two sea otters swam nearby.

By the end of the trip, everyone on the boat was in love with John, with the possible exception of a dog with a sun visor (now that was a rare sighting). Debarking was much easier than the steep embarking.

John hopped on his multi-colored pickup to change boots. I gladly put my sneakers back on, and they felt like heaven. I've never been hiking since in hip boots. They sit in the back of my closet stuffed with newspaper to keep them upright, and I wonder why I keep them.

After eating at a local restaurant, John decided to share his musical tastes with me. He played Russian Orthodox chants recorded in a church with a 9-second resonance. How, I wondered, did he come to know about this recording? How many sides did this man have? He couldn't have listened to recorded music at Murder Lake. He did mention that he had a radio . . . must have been battery-run. John Ireland—the man of mystery. The more I learned, the more I wondered.

Journal, August 11

Slept hard till 7:30. Beady eyes upon wakening. Ate fruit, tea, and oatmeal, which John offered to serve me in the lid of a rice pot, but I opted for a mug instead.

Then came another surprise. This man was not going to change his life even if he had a guest. He told me he was going trap shooting. I told him I would use the time to do some laundry. John asked me to wash some of his things if I was going to use the machines in the building. "Sure," I agreed. I wondered what he'd give me, since he had worn the same pair of pants and wool plaid shirt the entire time he was with me. He brought me two t-shirts, one pair of boxer shorts, and one pair of socks. Each, I noted, had a certain measure of renown. When he left for trap shooting, he wore the same pants and shirt he had worn at Murder Lake.

Before I could do the laundry, I needed quarters, so I got my coat and backpack and I was out as well. Walking around town, I stopped in a Ptarmigan Arts but bought nothing. I did remember to return to Toby Tyler's, where I bought a ground dogwood picture and a post card, carefully calculating that my change would produce quarters. There was a new-age herbal kind of place, where I bought a patch for my backpack, and asked for more quarters. Then, to my shame, I stopped at the only chain food place in the whole town, a Subway, and bought a sandwich and . . . . a Diet Coke! Was anybody watching?

I returned to John's apartment and started the laundry. While soap met clothing for the first time in over a week, I sketched various interesting objects in the apartment: John's stitching horse, an object I had never seen before or since, and his round knife (called an ulu in native culture) and the sheath he had made for it. My goodness, it seemed a long time for John to be gone. So I walked outside for a bit after the laundry was finished. There was a "big" music festival going on. Tom Bodett was there, and a lone Native American down by the water playing a flute. I phoned home. The call cost 10 cents.

John was still not home when I returned, so I picked up a book about Native Americans and started to read. When John finally returned, he was disgusted with his shooting. "I usually shoot 90 per—cent," he said. "Today I shot 75 percent."

By this time, after so many shared meals, I called myself "Potato Girl." I was routinely in charge of peeling while John cooked the rest, usually fish. Newspapers were used for tablecloths, and hotplates were old magazines or pieces of plywood. Pie tins served as plates. The halibut couldn't have tasted better if it had been served on fine china in a five-star restaurant.

That night's musical treat was Russian folk music. That was new to me, but tolerable. Then John asked, "Have you ever heard of Zamphir, master of the pan flute?" It was all I could do to stifle my laughter. "Oh, yes!" My son and I had a family joke about the "master," who frequently advertised on late night TV. "Yes! You can own this beautiful music if you order RIGHT NOW!" Now I had finally found someone who took this music seriously, and I couldn't believe it. John must have sensed something in my answer, for he didn't play it. I wrote in my journal, *I have got to make this man some new tapes.*

As we listened to the music, John brought out a box of photographs and invited me to look at them. The pictures had been sent to him by others, obviously, since he did not own a camera. They were mostly people pictures, taken by hunters and fishermen he had guided, and a few winter scenes, and fewer of animals. After I found the one of John with John Denver, I realized that John Ireland was quite a celebrity himself, at least in Alaska.

The story was repeated in detail. John Denver had visited the lodge near John's cabin at Murder Lake. A TV channel had made a video of the event, and it had aired some time ago. Months later, John sent me a copy of the video, which I copied before returning it to him.

The show was called Hillary's (as in Edmund Hillary) Adventurers; the segment was about the bush pilots of Alaska. John Denver went to Alaska for three days training in how to fly a float plane. His teacher, a bush pilot named Kathy, flew him into the Talkeetnas, and it sure looked like they landed on Murder Lake. Wearing hip boots, they waded ashore, Denver carrying his guitar. The video shows a few of Denver's lessons, then switches to "after school" activities: and there was John Ireland and John Denver, fishing from a canoe. John Ireland was not mentioned by name, instead, the narrator intoned, "A genuine love for the outdoors endeared him (Denver) to *this old man* (John Ireland). In this environment there's no discrimination between celebrity and *hermit*—only mutual respect and an enjoyment of the adventure to be found in nature."

The following day John readied for his appointment for muffler repair. He looked through many piles of papers trying to locate his checkbook. This proved to be a more difficult task for him than finding a walking stick hidden three years before, in the middle of the woods. When he finally found it, he remarked, "I used to have 'John Ireland, Murder Lake', printed on my checks. When a recipient asked for an explanation, I replied, 'I'm the only one who lives there *now*.'"

While John attended to his pick-up, I wandered around a supermarket (on Tuesdays, seniors got a 10% discount), had a quick look around a bookstore, and attempted to make travel arrangements to return to Anchorage so I could catch my flight home. The bus I had traveled on the previous year (and on which I had met John) was no longer in operation, so I ended up spending the grand sum of $59 for a flight from Homer to Anchorage.

We met up, as previously arranged, at the antique store, and off we went in a newly quiet pick-up. John handed me a bag of Bull Durham tobacco. "It's the best thing in the world to clean your windshield. Hang it in your car." I did, but I never used it.

That day John and I had lunch at the senior center, and that day we had more than just food—we listened to an Athabasca story teller, who told Native American legends. How the walrus got whiskers: A walrus went on land and tried to eat a porcupine, and of course, got quills in his cheeks. He vowed never to go on land again, and retreated to the water repeating, "O that hurts."

Next we visited the long-term care unit at the local hospital. My journal reads, *"Some charismatic Bible-thumping too, too sweet females were there who sang, hugged, and gave out cookies with 'teachings' on them. They gave the patients tambourines, bells, and maracas to accompany their sincere singing. By the time a Ms. Grateful-to-God was half way through the teaching, everyone in the room was asleep except for me and the blind lady next to me."*

Before John and I left, we took a turn around the garden. John disappeared into the trees to "water the lilies." When he returned, he was holding a rutabaga. On the way back to John's place on (what else) Main Street, we saw a young boy standing in the middle of the street. John called out, "You'll have to hang a license plate on your backside if you want to stay there."

Journal, August 13

Dismal day. So rainy we did not walk. John went to the mental health annex to work on a horse-shoe pit and dropped me at Pratt museum. I sinned again by slipping off to the Subway to enjoy a Diet Pepsi.

Not much was going on in the town of Homer. Homeroids, as some people call them, are quiet-living folks. I thought I'd try walking away from the stores. Climbing a hill beyond John's apartment, I spied a little park. It became my destination. I had enough time to complete two sketches before the sky became so overcast I thought I'd better go indoors before I got soaked. Back in the apartment I drew a piece of leatherworking equipment called a stripper. John appeared, satisfied with his horse-shoe performance. He had made the only ringer.

We split a beer and John brought out his animal sketches that had not been printed in his book. It was clear to me that he didn't need a camera—so skillful was his drawing. His animals showed life and movement. I vowed to loosen up my own rather stiff drawings, but alas, it never happened.

Next on John's agenda was archery. I don't know where that was done. He came, he went, and didn't offer much explanation. When he returned, we had our usual snack of rye tack, cheese, and pecans. Then we flossed our teeth together, he brushed his hearing aids, and prepared for bed. I managed to blurt, "I don't know how I can adequately thank you." He replied, matter-of-factly, "Not necessary. I wouldn't have gone up there alone. It wouldn't have been so amusing to me. I like to have someone to teach. I'm just glad you took so much pleasure in seeing Alaska." So the moment passed, and I crawled into my sleeping bag.

The following morning we had rice and raisins for breakfast. John began talking about how women seemed to like him. I was preparing to yawn when he said, "But you are the best." My face turned red. He went on to say if I ever got a job teaching in Alaska we could live together and share rent (!) He said he was surprised how easy it was to be with me. I didn't "irritate" him. What could I say to that? I was struck dumb.

We had spoken about a book called <u>Solitude,</u> by Anthony Storr. John didn't have a copy of it, so he suggested we walk to the public library so he could show it to me and he could borrow a copy. He also wanted me to copy out a quote from Wordsworth, so he could post it on his kitchen cabinet. I love these lines:

> *When from our better selves we have too long*
> *been parted by the hurrying world, and droop,*
> *sick of its business, of its pleasure tired,*
> *how gracious, how benign, is solitude.*

We loaded up the pick-up and lunched at the senior center. One of the men there told me to come again next year. John told me to consider that a compliment. On the way to the airport, John began talking more and more, and I got quieter and quieter. A neat little Piper was waiting for me and three other people. Before I was allowed to board, the crew weighed my bags, and recorded my personal weight. My purse had to go in the wing. John gave me a big bear hug, and I was off.

Back in Anchorage, at the hotel, I felt discombobulated. The shower and clear towels and sheets were like heaven. I enjoyed watching T.V. It was a beautiful evening. Walking out to find dinner, I stopped outside a Native arts shop and stood entranced as Rossini's music was broadcast onto the sidewalks. I remembered a line from one of my favorite movies, Never Cry Wolf, taken from Farley Mowat's book of the same name:

"I want to say thank you, straight up to the universe."

Above John's Mt.
from Bayview Park
8-13-91
Homer, AK

5

Home looked good to me. But Alaska was an experience I would always cherish. How could I express my gratitude? John had told me about bush radio. In Alaska, bush radio is a method of communication for people who cannot use a telephone or other methods of communication. Remember, this was 1991, a mostly pre-internet era, pre-cell-phone era. Besides, many, many areas of Alaska are truly remote. Bush radio operated at certain times of the day, and could be received by anyone having a radio. People could send in requests to broadcast, and their messages would be sent out. John listened to bush radio every day, and I had heard broadcasts sending requests of people needing a ride from one place to another; people sending out pleas for help for a fishing boat or hunting party that was missing; people just wanting to say hello to family members away from traditional communications. I had jotted down the number and decided to phone in a message that would be sent, knowing that one day, John would hear it. The wording was carefully thought out. I decided on, "Thanks to John Ireland, for the gift of a true Alaskan experience."

That may or may not have been a good idea. The message was for John, but anyone who listened to bush radio heard it. Though John understood it, apparently some of his acquaintances gave the messages an entirely different, and unexpected, meaning. In his first letter to me after our visit, he said, ". . . *heard 'bush line' from you—grateful that you returned safely. I'm delighted that your experience with me was a peak in your life. I can't help but think you must have had a lot of dull times. That you indicated very high trust in me brings a feeling of warmth. Perhaps you perceived that I'm entirely guileless. And perhaps that's what disappoints me, in cases of some others, when they act like they think I have some hidden motives."*

When I had visited John's friends who were teachers, we talked about exchange teaching. I was eager to swap teaching positions with someone in Alaska, and began making overtures to my school board. For John had said, "If you indeed can arrange to transfer your teaching to this area, perhaps we can share more time together." My school board was entirely agreeable. The trick was to find someone in Alaska willing to swap jobs and housing for a year.

So our separate lives began anew, and our correspondence continued.

In 1976, I had begun to draw and print my own personal Christmas cards, and I continue the custom to this day. That year, I drew the interior of John's cabin, and instead of quotations posted around the room, I sketched in a string of cards like I had seen in his apartment. I sent one to him, along with some cassette tapes of music I thought he'd like. He commented that he did not send cards or give gifts, but he enjoyed mine. "What you do, you do well."

His seasonal greeting was, "Tis the season of peace and good will: time to kill a bird or a pig and a tree."

My son, who was in the Air Force repaying them with service for his university education, came home for Christmas. I had not seen him for a year. He reminded me of who I was. We went snorkeling and searched for the tiny Key Deer in the Keys, and tromped around Everglades National Park. That year, his gift for me was Norman MacLean's book, A River Runs Through It. The main character's fly casting instructions were exactly like those John had taught me. I was delighted.

The hours of light were growing short in Homer, and John, in his letters, seemed to display some depression. He wrote of feeling ill and being disgusted with world events. I could not imagine spending a winter in Alaska, though at that point I was still trying to arrange a teaching swap. I had lived two winters in Minneapolis, but I recall that city as much more sunny and cheerful, despite being cold, than places I had lived in Cleveland and Syracuse, where winters were gray.

In January, John wrote, *"So you had no answer from the University of Alaska (regarding teacher swap). Like it's becoming current practice to ignore letters of inquiry."* In February, he asked a friend of his on a local school board, for advice. Again, no response.

In his letters, John included descriptions of Alaskan winters:

". . . I trimmed my hair and beard this morning. I used to have to keep my beard short during winters at Murder Lake, as severely cold temps made a mess of condensation with icicles." . . . *"while out walking last evening, I was advanced upon by a cow moose which has been frequenting the area. An idiot lives across the street has been feeding the moose. This keeps them around. It is never sane policy to feed any large animal species which could inflict bodily injury. I avoided becoming too chummy with any large animals at Murder Lake. I only encouraged the jays and chickadees, in which cases I felt it would be amusing to have them fly up and perch on me."*

"We had coldest temps of winter this month (March); down to 5 below zero F. one night; then suddenly warmed to 46 above today. Melt water running along sides of streets. I swept accumulation of snow off my truck before it would maybe freeze on a thick mass, hard to remove. I haven't been driving for more than a month."

"Weather is fine (April). Slight frost overnight. Been sunny and warm during days—'shirtsleeve weather.' The roads are clear of snow and ice. I could start using the pickup again."

Meanwhile, my life went on in its usual fashion: working at my teaching job, fulfilling my daughterly duties by regularly visiting my aging mother, and my motherly duties by following my son's activities in the Air Force. John frequently remarked that he did not know how I found time to write. His correspondence was one of the great pleasures in my life.

He wrote of continuing with his many activities: saw and scissor-sharpening, making a longbow, leather work, trap shooting, even clam-digging in the spring, about which he said, "I'm not a very good clam-digger, nor a very good clam cook."

The book John had written, his book about his wilderness experiences, was called The Friendly Wilderness. Before it had been published, KBBI radio station in Homer asked him to read it on air, which he did. Kachemak Horizons had made a cassette tape of the broadcast. John sent me a copy. I played it for my first grade class.

Chapter 1 was about Gray Jays . . . "which are also called a variety of different names, including Canada Jay, Camp Robber, and Whisky Jack, which is a corruption of the name by which Indians called them—wees-ka-chon." When John first moved into the wilderness, he set up a length of log like a stump and placed food scraps on it. It became sort of a game, John tried to keep food on the stump and the Jays worked to keep it cleared. Twenty-some years later, when I visited the cabin on Murder Lake, the jays were still cleaning up for us after we fished.

In April, we were both still working on exchange teaching opportunities for me. John was beginning to experience a few tourists arriving; I was observing the exodus of snowbirds and looking forward to a jaunt to North Carolina with an old friend of mine. I love Florida, but there's something exhilarating about mountains, and they were calling to me.

So off I went. Wildflowers were everywhere at low elevations, though there was still some snow in the mountains. Dogwoods and apple trees were blooming, and carpets of violets were everywhere.

Shy, hopeful trilliums were popping up. One day while we were enjoying a peaceful view from an overlook on the Blue Ridge Parkway, we were joined by a man and his two young sons. I judged them to be about 5 and 7 years old. The man sat down on the ground but the two boys hopped about boisterously. The man said, "Can't you kids just sit still and enjoy the scenery and be thankful for your blessings?" The youngest one replied, "We're just so thankful you're out of work, daddy, and can bring us up here!" The man got kind of a grim look on his face and muttered, "Get in the car, kids."

A casual invitation arrived in May: *"Hey, you think about coming to AK this summer vacation? You're welcome at my place, and perhaps to Murder Lake, like ca. Aug. 7. By the way, Lee plans to build a pre-cut cabin on the place this summer; the prospect is distasteful to me."*

Tempting as the offer was, there were other events in my life. My son was returning to the States after flying all over Europe for two months. And, to my joy, he planned to marry that summer. His fiancée was a wonderful girl and I would not miss the wedding for anything. Maybe I could juggle travel arrangements before school began again. The idea of "improvements" to John's property on Murder Lake, though, was not attractive to me. Some places are so perfect in memory that one doesn't want to "go back." Perhaps it's better to let them stay in happy memories.

My son set the date for August 8. My nephew was to marry in late August. I was expected to attend, with my mother. For my birthday (June), my mother offered to buy us air tickets to England. She was 82, and she wanted to visit our family again before she became too old to travel. Our family was scattered from Yorkshire to Cornwall. It would take some time. I couldn't juggle or afford all these. It was just as well. Hurricane Andrew struck in late August, and that caused major upheavals. Clearly, the fates decided when I should follow the pull back to Alaska. The possibility of exchange teaching died at this point as well. Someone in the Homer school board told John that they'd back off from hiring a good, experienced teacher because they'd have to pay more, so instead they would hire one just out of school to learn on the job.

I asked if I could visit Alaska the following summer and John responded enthusiastically. He said we could go back to Murder Lake. By November plans were already in motion. By April, I had made my air reservations to Anchorage. We'd mutually agreed on a week at Murder Lake. Lee once again, agreed to fly us up and back. I cooked up a plan to travel from Anchorage by train to Seward; spend two nights there, then take a ferry to Homer, where I'd meet up with John for the week at Murder Lake. I wondered if the site could ever be the same with Lee's pre-cut cabin on it.

And then . . . John got a job offer! A caretaker/watchman was needed at a logging camp in a place called Koyuktolik (Dogfish) Bay. A foreign corporation was looking to buy the property, and there was some uncertainty about the original Aleutic timber rights. Meanwhile, the camp had been vacated. Equipment and housing was on site and there was concern about theft and deterioration. A man younger than John decided he couldn't take the solitude, so John "jumped right on it."

"We could visit there. I'd be alone at the camp. Must be an airstrip there, served by any of several air charter services, such as one owned by a friend. We'd be by a beach, fishing for salmon instead of rainbows. I understand this camp has 'luxuries' like electric power from a diesel generator, refrigerator, radio as well as T.V., and telephone. I need you to set me straight on some of these contrivances. What would you think of that? I do not want to turn down this opportunity. I'd love to escape."

Well! I jumped right on THAT! Another adventure! I wrote a quick response, but John didn't receive it until he was already at Dogfish Bay, where the mail was forwarded from Homer once weekly by a bush pilot. Now John's letters were scrawled long-hand, as he had left his Underwood in Homer. The messages came through quite clearly, though. He set a day for his friend to fly me into the camp. The beach was used as a landing strip.

Shortly after John got situated at Dogfish Bay, some of the "luxuries" gave out. *The diesel generator quit. I was without phone to let them know, as generator powers the phone—also no heat, lights, or water. But I improvised and made out. No kind of back up for even cooking. I dug a military type toilet facility and cooked with scraps of wood picked up around the smoke house. It rained four days so I put up a shed against the front of the smokehouse so I could stand under it and cook. There must be a back up for toilet and cooking/heat if I'd stay over winter.*"

It was a bit tricky to get help without a working phone. John knew what to do. He went down to the shore and hand signaled to a passing boat. Two hours later, so he said, a Coast Guard helicopter from Kodiak landed on the beach to learn what was wrong.

So repairs were made while John spent a few days back in Homer, and then a letter arrived saying all was well. He gave me the phone number, but as a back up, he also gave me the number of the radio station to call for "Bushlines," which he planned to listen to five times daily. He didn't plan to be within earshot of the phone all the time. I reminded myself not to send any messages that could be misinterpreted by listeners!

I was advised to bring wellies instead of hip boots, warm clothes, and rain gear. He requested some provisions from town, especially a certain brand of mosquito repellent. He ordered groceries by the month, so he said he could always use fresh vegetables, fruit, and eggs. Then, in his last letter, he closed with *"Heard a plane, maybe chance to mail out."* It was then that I resolved to ask my mom to send a letter to the camp while I was there, so I could receive mail sent in by bush pilot, just to add more spice to this next adventure.

6

Plan in place, I boarded an airplane on July 26, 1993, to begin another Alaskan adventure. Fort Lauderdale to Seattle to Anchorage, and then I was once again comfortably ensconced in the Anchorage Hotel.

The next morning there was a newspaper outside the door to my room. McDonald's advertised a "McKinley Mac" and Dominos recommended a "Domino Dominator"—a pizza too big for their delivery bags.

Not having a current bus schedule in hand, I went directly to 7th and Gambell to visit the Seward Bus Line office. A surly woman grudgingly sold me a ticket from Homer to Anchorage for my return, and did not disguise her disgust at my declaration that I would be carrying two duffle bags. Mission accomplished.

It was a beautiful day. Twice I sat for long periods in Elderberry Park. Denali was almost visible, or at least I so imagined. I sketched Cook Inlet. Lunch was a Diet Pepsi and a pack of peanut butter crackers. I noted that bananas were 75 cents each. What a great feeling it is to be away from home in a place so different, where no one knows you, and there is no schedule to be met. No conversation required.

The Alaska Public Lands Information Center proved to be an excellent diversion. I viewed a free film about the Alaska Highway and how it was built. The road had been planned for years, but not until World War II did it seem a crucial project. Many black "service corps" served by being laborers. Imagine, being from the southern U.S. and ending up in the Alaskan harsh climate, working in mud, snow, and ice, under dark skies. One G.I. was quoted as saying, "This place is just miles and miles of nothing but miles and miles!"

After a fine halibut dinner, I returned to the Center to hear a naturalist speak about puffins, murres, and auks, which I expected to see on another leg of my journey.

In my journal that night, I wrote, *"I feel completely happy."*

The next morning I was at the train station at 6:30. Who should I meet in line but another single woman traveler, Lynn, a jewelry designer from Pompano Beach, who was *camping* across Alaska. Pompano is about 15 minutes from my home.

I had been looking forward to this train journey, for on my first trip to Alaska with Rosemary, we had ridden this route in a single car train—which seemed to us quite unique. It was. This time the train had three cars. "It's difficult to repeat experiences", I thought. However, the scenery was as stunning as it was three years ago: Through mountain passes, across tidal flats, and through virgin forests we saw glaciers, waterfalls, wildflowers and wildlife. It was sensational.

The train arrived in Seward at 11:30, but my room wouldn't be "available" until 4 o'clock. I dumped my bags and went for a walk.

Journal—July 28

Averting eyes from shop windows, I walked to Two Lakes Trail. Pretty woodsy trail around—you guessed it—two lakes. Saw Stellar Jays and was able to photograph them since they are not timid at all.

I returned from my walk to find a note from my new friend Lynn asking me to walk over to her tent and perhaps go to dinner with her. So I did. It was raining by then, and I was hard put to imagine her sleeping in a tent alone. It didn't seem to bother her.

After the meal, Lynn and I went to a small building for a slide show about the Iditerod Trail for sled dog racing. Remember, this was years before Power Point presentations. A long-bearded man from Iowa ran the slide projector. A predecessor of a techie had produced the show, and had included an audible signal to let the projectionist know when to change the slide. What was the signal? A dog's bark. "Yip! Yip!" Time to move on to the next picture. Lynn and I were shaking with giggles by the end of the program.

Journal—July 29

What a day! A day to remember for a lifetime.

I had arranged to spend the day on a boat trip south out of Seward around Kenai Fjords National Park, in advance of my meet up with John. We set off in fog and rain. Alaska mornings are often like this, and then, like the start of a stage performance, the rain stops, and the curtain of fog rises to reveal mountains, waterfalls, sun-lit seas, glaciers, and wildlife. Orcas breached and tail-lobbed. Sea otters swam on their backs, eating abalone. Harbor seals lazed on rocks. Puffins, kittiewakes, and gulls flew about. Cormorants and murres perched on rocks near the water, while bald eagles sat high in spruces waiting for hunting opportunities. We passed Bear Glacier and as we paused at Holgate Glacier, we heard it calve with a booming "crack!" It was Alaska at its finest.

Lynn came after me that evening and asked me to go to the Yukon Bar with her. I socialized for a bit and left for my digs about eleven. A nearly full moon was rising over Resurrection Bay as a grand finale to the day.

The following day presented itself as usual: fog. I struck off for the Chamber of Commerce to see what I could see, for my ferry to

Kodiak/Homer, the Tustumena, did not depart until 8 p.m. The kind volunteer at the Chamber gave me the key to St. Peter's Episcopal Church so that I could see a noted mural painted by the Dutch artist, Jan Van Emple. That's trust! By the time I returned the key, the sun was shining through the clouds, so I took off for Marathon Mountain. This is the site of a race for sturdy folks. I figured if they could run up and down this mountain, I could at least walk it. Wrong. It is very steep. I started up, then after reconsideration, turned back and discovered the only way I felt comfortable going down was on my backside. I decided the preferred activity for me was to sit on a rock and sketch the mountain. While I worked, a young woman with a dog trotted easily up the mountain and disappeared. After a while, I headed back to town with a decent drawing and a muddy rear end . . . and a big smile.

Next stop was the Seward Library, where I saw a movie and slides about the 1964 earthquake. While there, I found a book called Northern Christmas, by the artist and writer Rockwell Kent. I had not known that Kent had spent some time in Alaska. He had found inspiration in the wilderness and illustrated Resurrection Bay with many pen and ink drawings.

Lynn and I were booked on the same ferry. I had reserved a cabin, for the trip to Kodiak/Homer would take most of two days and two nights. The cabin had bunk beds, so I offered to share with Lynn.

I copied this quotation from her hat:

> "Travel is fatal to prejudice, bigotry, and narrow-mindedness, and many of our people need it sorely. Broad, wholesome, charitable views cannot be acquired by vegetating in one's little corner of earth."
>
> Mark Twain, 1869

Next morning, she bought me breakfast in return for the bunk aboard the Tustumena. A teacher from Vermont joined us for scrambled eggs, toast, juice and coffee. She showed us an article that had appeared in the Alaska Daily News. It remains one of the funniest articles I have ever read, and I quote it here:

Georgia Dog Joins Alaska Food Chain, by Marilee Enge

> *In the land of magnificent beasts and great struggles between civilization and nature, a pair of elderly tourists in a Winnebago found out just how cruel nature can be.*
>
> *The Georgia husband and wife were wiping the windshield of their freshly washed motor home at the New Town Chevron station in Valdez a week ago Monday. Their tiny dog ran in circles near its mistress's feet. Nearby, Dennis Fleming pumped propane for a customer.*
>
> *As Fleming watched in astonishment, a bald eagle that keeps a perch above the downtown gas station spread its great wings and dove to the pavement below.*
>
> *'The dog was no more than five feet from the lady,' Fleming recalled. 'The eagle swooped down and grabbed the dog with both of its talons. The dog let out a half yelp.' The hound couldn't have known what hit it.*
>
> *'The eagle just crushed it,' Fleming said. 'His head limped to the side.'*
>
> *With 5 or 6 pounds of 'Chihuahua-type' meat in its talons, the eagle soared out over the bay.*
>
> *The horrified woman could only say, 'Oh my God.' Then she began to cry and her husband came around the camper to comfort her, Fleming said. She cried on his shoulder a while.*
>
> *Fleming said he tried to help console the woman and she asked him if the eagle's behavior was normal. Then she got in the passenger seat and her husband walked around the vehicle.*
>
> *As soon as he was out of his wife's sight, Fleming watched a big smile break out on the man's face. He clenched his fists in a victory gesture. 'Yeah, yeah,' he said.*

Then, sober faced, the husband got in the driver's seat and the couple drove off.

Shortly after breakfast, the ferry docked at Kodiak Island. Lynn planned to camp there, and soon she was chatting up a man for advice. The woman could talk easily to anyone with no qualms about being misunderstood. When we were in the Yukon Bar, she drank only coffee yet left the bar with an invitation to go out on some stranger's boat. She wore black tights and a t-shirt, and some fringed boots. Her vest was covered with pins from everywhere she had been. She was a thoroughly pleasant and unique person.

I left her to her tenting site exploration and went off to photograph the beautiful Russian Orthodox Church, with its blue dome and interesting cross. After calling in at the Baranov Museum, I boarded the ferry again and waited for supper time. I was happy to take a table by myself and read a book while I ate, comparing myself to the sociable and gregarious Lynn.

Near 11 that night, the pink sky was darkening; arctic winds blew across the bow of the ferry. Humpback whales were all around. It was thrilling to watch them breach, spout, then dive with a flip of their magnificent tails.

The ferry reached Homer around 2:30 a.m. A comfy, warm room was waiting for me there. I snoozed and prepared to meet up with my friend John. The bush pilot was due to pick me up early afternoon, so I briefly visited the little town. Although the Subway and grocery store that I recalled were still there, alas, "Family Dinning" was no more. On John's request, I filled a cardboard box with fresh fruit, cheese, rye tack, broccoli and tomatoes, and lugged it back to my room. I sat on the steps with the box and my luggage and waited for George, the pilot.

Journal, August 1, 1995

So . . . here came George, right on time. Dusty old car—zipped out to air strip on the Spit. Cessna. Love it! Just rapt during the

flight. Tongue hanging out. Saw Redoubt and Iliamna volcanoes;
Augustine (volcano) cloud-covered. Beautiful blue water. Great day.

The tiny, solitary figure of John grew larger as we approached
the beach. Was he wearing the same brown plaid shirt and brown
trousers he wore at Murder Lake?? He welcomed me to Dogfish
Bay with a big hug, and zip—George was gone. Wind blew through
the spruce. Waves whooshed on the shore. I was once again in the
wilderness.

This wilderness had been scarred by mankind, though.
Although the area had not been clear-cut, beautiful, large trees had
been selectively logged. Roads had been cut through the forest, and
heavy equipment was scattered around the site. An ugly (but useful)
$50,000 incinerator stood off from the other buildings. When the
camp was in use, there had been far too much refuse for gray jays
to clean up! A kitchen building still contained some supplies, logs
were stacked by giant saws, and the trailer John lived in was not
as picturesque as his little cabin, for sure. The outhouse John had
constructed next to the trailer was the only rough building. A beat
up truck was parked next to the trailer. Inside the trailer were a
satellite phone, a television, an actual bathroom, and a washer and
drier. The kitchen was furnished with a refrigerator and stove,
which ran off the generator. One could still walk a short distance
and feel the remoteness of the place. Down at the beach, in the
mornings, coyote tracks were clearly visible, and sea otters frolicked
in the surf. The spruce trees were full of little yellow warblers
feeding on the cones. Eagles caught thermals above. Wildflowers

were everywhere, just waiting for me to come along with my pencil and sketch pad, it seemed. Fish jumped in the sloughs formed at high tides (at full moon, could be 19 feet). Looking across the bay toward Mt. Douglas, I sometimes saw black bears running about.

After my arrival, we went down to the beach to fish. It did not seem like two years had passed by since I had seen John. He was easy company, once again, and I continued to pay careful attention to his advice. Creature comforts were available, but we were still in the wilderness. We did no fly casting this time, and had no luck, either, so we resorted to a meal of sausage, potatoes (for which I automatically assumed responsibility), onion, and broccoli, washed down with tea.

The television at Dogfish Bay received Rural Alaska Television, affectionately called RATNET. The station gave weather reports, flying forecasts (VFR, visual flight rule; MVFR, marginal visual rule; and IFR, instrument flight rule), freezing levels, and all sorts of information necessary to those living remotely, or those planning to go to remote areas. We needed to pay attention to these reports to know if the bush pilot would be able to pick me up on the day I was slated to return to Homer.

John's first morning responsibility was to check the generators on site. There was a small gasoline generator, which John cranked up, then switched the phone to that power. Then he turned off the big diesel generator, checked it, and reversed the procedure. All worked well that morning.

Blueberries were everywhere, much to John's delight, so we went berry picking. We also picked salmonberries. At Murder Lake, John had recommended them as juiciest of all the berries. They became my favorite. John said the natives came here to pick berries, and I might one day meet some of them. The whole time I stayed at Dogfish Bay, no matter how far we roamed from the camp (we walked for hours), I never did see where they lived, but I did meet some who visited by boat.

That night I took a shower! I felt a little like I had the better of two worlds.

After the clouds and fog lifted the next morning, we prepared for a day of hiking. We walked along a logging road up to the timberline through fireweed, alders, and spruce. A fox sparrow was eating salmonberries. John said, "good bear country," but we didn't see any. He did identify coyote scat, full of salmonberry seeds. So I was not alone in my fondness for them! John found some berries from twisted stalk, called watermelon berries. If a person knew what he was doing, he could survive quite a while grazing off this land. The day was beautiful, warm enough in the sun, but cool in the shade. Perfect for walking. We skirted around two hornet nests and found a place to sit and have lunch. After walking for five hours, we were back at the camp, and made a distressing discovery. The toilet in the trailer would not flush. Good thing John had constructed that outhouse!

Phone calls were made. On the advice of the manager, John started digging under a waterfall to find the pipe leading to a settling tank (he was told it had a yellow rope on it), which led to the water filter and pump, as it might be clogged. This 78-year-old man dug gravel and heavy mud for two hours. When I voiced concern regarding the difficulty of the work, he said, "Well, I haven't done anything today . . . just walk."

And there I was, sitting on a rock, panting, from walking for five hours. I sat and drew wildflowers and expected him to drop over at any moment. I did in fact offer to help, and once did run back to the pump house to check the water level, but he refused my offer of digging assistance (thank goodness). At 8 o'clock, after no luck finding the pipe, he decided to quit. I cooked dinner while he rested, and we kept the water pump on "off" and used the outhouse.

The previous evening's shower was the only one I ever had at Dogfish Bay. Not having modern conveniences such as running water is one thing. Having a convenience such as water pouring forth from a tap and then suddenly <u>not</u> having it is completely different.

FIREWEED

At Murder Lake, John had gathered wonderful water every day from the spring by the lake. The bay was salt water. He quickly rigged a way to gather rain water, but the waterfall and creek remained our main source of water, and that had to be carried some distance, then boiled. So much for the shower and washer in the trailer. Back to basics. Every day became a quest to repair the water system, quench thirst, and try to stay clean.

The following morning, John, after hours of digging, finally found the fabled settling tank box with the yellow rope. He tried back-flushing the filter. The pump started overworking and the reservoir was still not filling from the creek. So . . . we had lunch. John decided to make more phone calls seeking advice for a repair.

I wasn't much use to him in the digging gravel department, so I asked if I could go off berry-picking. He said, "Remember, bears like berries, too. I don't suppose it would do much good to give you a gun to carry." He was so right. Guns and I are not friends. We really hadn't seen any bears nearby, so off I went. I had to keep an eye out for Devil's Club as well as bears. Devil's Club is a huge plant with large thorns. It was an interesting experience to be picking berries while hearing surf in the near distance. A Stellar Jay scolded me briefly. I must have been gone too long, for John came looking for me after a while. He was carrying his hand gun.

Nothing John did seemed to increase the water intake to the reservoir. He shut it off for the night.

Journal, August 5, Dogfish Bay

Oh, my, it was down in the 40's yesterday in Homer, so the TV said. It is so weird to wake up and hear John stomp around to put on the TV. It's so out of character. Today's weather looks more like the Alaska I remember. Totally foggy and cold.

Morning brought the same plumbing woes. I had been traveling for nine days by now, so I asked John if I could do some laundry in a bucket. He agreed. Here is reason number one why smart people do not travel in Alaska wearing jeans. Fortunately, I was smart enough. Fast drying lighter pants worn with thin, Patagonia underwear, are every bit as warm as denim, and much easier to launder.

I hung my small amount of laundry to dry and went looking for less of a survival endeavor. John had pointed out chamomile plants growing between the sidewalk blocks. He described it as a plant that liked to be walked upon—"it grows where you walk." In Alaska, it is called pineapple weed because it smells like pineapple. I drew a little sketch of it and noted some comments. After I completed my sketch, I crushed a bit of it and sniffed. True, it did remind me of pineapple.

Before we had lunch I checked out my laundry. It seemed clean and odor-free.

Then John said, "It seems like a feller should do something." What did that mean? It meant that we were back at the waterfall, and, perhaps out of desperation, John decided to teach me how to shovel gravel. "Don't shovel crossways." John shoveled like a 20-year-old and I did my best, which wasn't exactly expert assistance. I believe that John wished to be a problem-solver in my eyes, and in the eyes of his employer, but it wasn't to be.

A day can be spent performing ordinary chores that at home would occupy only an hour. I asked, and was granted, water from the creek below the waterfall, to take a bath that night. At least I could stand in a bathtub and wash. We gathered drinking water in a pail. Since the pail was an integral part of our rain-collecting apparatus, John found a different container from the kitchen building to use for my bath water. Unfortunately, the container had a clearly legible label attached to it reading "FRYMAX." It reeked of the remains of strong cooking oil. Washing the container did little to remove the smell. It was awful, trying to bathe in water that smelled like rancid lard. Luckily, I had snatched a cup from the kitchen in the trailer, put some boiled water in it straight from the kettle, saved it in my room, and used it to cleanse the "sensitive areas" of my body.

Next day, the Alaska climate provided water for us. It rained all day.

Journal, August 6

Washed socks and underwear in the last of the rancid fat water. At 11:48 p.m., my laundry was still not dry, after being in the drier for 20 minutes and then hung indoors all day with the heat on.

I remembered a trip to Belize, when I washed socks in the jungle. My room had generator-provided electricity only until 11 p.m. each day. I hung my socks from a ceiling fan which rotated three days before the socks were dry. Humidity is a factor in both cold and hot climates!

John amazed me by being attentive to junk on TV. He reminded me of my ex-husband, who declared he hated TV, but if it happened to be on, he could not take his eyes from it. John watched a Robin Hood movie and Kung Fu. I opted to snuggling into my blanket in my room.

The following morning I slept until 8 a.m. When I emerged from my room, John opined, "I thought you might be ill."

It was a blustery day. The wind was straight out of the north all day. White caps frothed on the bay. Gulls cried over the huge surf.

John donned a cap before venturing outdoors. It was a black cap with the word "nothing" on it. When I questioned him about it, he said, "At the Salvation Army, I was looking for a cap with nothing on it. One of my friends overheard my request and brought me this one."

He "had a notion" to "lie next to the earth." I followed him down to the beach, where he lay down in the fireweed and other wildflowers. Out of the wind, it was quite warm and peaceful. I left him to it. I wondered if he was feeling the effects of the heavy shoveling, or if he was sick. I had asked him once what happened to a person in the wilderness if he were to get sick. He replied, "You don't get sick." Had he left the wilderness because he had been diagnosed with an illness? He didn't take any medications. Perhaps I was just imagining things.

During my stay at Dogfish Bay, I decided that each day I would pick up a rock. I never see rocks in Florida; only sand, shells, and cement residue. The rocks in Alaska are beautiful—striated and colorful. I still have the rocks I picked up, and when I roll them over in my hands, I relive my time at Dogfish Bay. So I went about looking for "the perfect rock" and enjoyed watching a sparrow hawk chasing a little warbler, ravens flying about, just breathing in Alaska air.

Alaskans are so casual about visiting by bush plane. It continued to amaze me. Two visitors arrived that day, via George and Gulf Air. They had been instructed to post legal notices on the property. The notices said that Eagle Bay natives were not responsible to pay workers for work done on this property. This was all a mystery to me. While John talked business with the visitors, George and I discussed various subjects, like the tracks I had seen on the beach. He declared that cats retract their claws when they walk and dogs do not. This would be an aid to identifying animal tracks. He further said that it was quite unusual that there were not 50 or 60 mountain goats wandering about.

That night, probably out of boredom, and to continue his role of teacher, John began to show me how to tie various knots. This brought back many memories of my boating days with my husband. We owned a little sailboat, and I had many lessons about knot-tying, most of which I had forgotten. Why, why, why, I wondered, did I always end up striving to be approved by a man for being skillful in areas which did not really interest me? I can still do a proper half-hitch and square knot, but forget bowline and clove hitch. How often does one need to know those? If I can tie up an orchid plant or bird feeder in my back yard, and tie the bow of a boat to a dock, that's all I think I need to know. I still don't remember under what conditions one needs a bowline. All I can recall is something about a rabbit running out of the hole, and then back into it.

Journal, August 8, Dogfish Bay

The plan was to shovel gravel this morning. After lunch, John amazed me again by hearing two ATV's approach while we were watching the Buick Open Golf Tournament. There were four Natives: the Chief of English Bay, his wife, and their two sons. They seemed to be shy, kindly people. The Chief smoked Camels. He reported seeing goats nearby.

The conversation seemed rather formal, and must have been somewhat important in maintaining good relationships between the Natives and the logging company John represented. I don't remember what was said after the goat report, for at that moment I was astonished to see that there was a dead fly in John's beard. That, I remember. Does one tell a person that there is a dead fly in his beard? In front of company? I turned away to make tea for John's guests and lost the conversation and stifled a smile. By the time I served the tea, the fly was gone.

Later that afternoon, events improved. The day proved to be windy, but clear and sunny. We walked to the slough, which the native chief had called a lagoon. There was a small fishing boat anchored there. I cast enthusiastically using a small spoon which John called a Pixee. I caught two terribly ugly fish called Irish Lords. Then—wow! Something grabbed my lure, and John was glad to provide coaching. Rod tip up! Steady reeling! A Dolly Varden trout! As soon as I had landed it on the rocks, it shook loose from the lure. John was at the ready with a rock to kill it. Sixteen inches! This was a lot more fun than shoveling gravel, for both of us.

The Dolly Varden Trout is named after a beautiful, lively, and brightly dressed girl in Dickens' Barnaby Rudge. It was, indeed, aptly named, a beautiful sight, shining on the banks. It proved to be as tasty as it was pretty.

That evening, as we took the fish guts down to the beach for the birds, we found that at some point that day, a plane had delivered a new water pump for John to install. While we were figuring out how to carry it back to the trailer, eagles came to eat the fish guts. I made a mistake. I ran back to the trailer to get my camera. By the time I returned to the beach, everything was gone. I vowed to remember my son's advice: First, watch. Then, if there's time, grab the camera.

The next day we started up an old diesel pick-up truck and drove it close to the beach so we could pick up the heavy pump and take it to the settling tank. We worked nearly all day on the water system, using the new pump to try to clear the settling tank. Pump, pump, wait. Pump, pump, wait. A lot of silt and muck came out, and finally, late in the afternoon, we found the intake pipe sitting loose in the muck. I made a slip knot (as instructed) to make a noose and we snagged it. So that's why knowing how to tie knots is useful! However, this proved to be the only occasion in my life, so far, that I needed to snag an intake pipe from muck. John hurried to the phone to report our progress. He reckoned we could stop work for the day and enjoy berry picking. While we picked, I saw, a pine grosbeak for the first time. He was eating the berries from a Devil's Club. That cheerful red bird ended up on my Christmas card that year.

The respite was happy, but brief. Upon our return to the trailer, the camp manager phoned to say he needed to pick up the old pump the following day, so that left a task for the morning.

I bathed and washed my hair with a bucket of rainwater. John was asleep when I finished. My journal read, *"I practiced tying knots until I was in knots."*

This visit was certainly different from Murder Lake. For one thing, we had many more visitors. One day George flew in two men to "evaluate" the logs that had been cut, but were still lying about, some a good distance from the trailer, on the logging road. They were gone a long time because they had a flat tire. That's one mishap John and I had avoided. George picked up any mail before he made the flight to Dogfish. The day the "log auditors" (what else can you call them?) came, he brought a letter for me. My mom came through. I was thrilled to receive a letter brought by a bush pilot! George and I spent some time together while he waited to make the return trip. We sat on the beach and he helped me identify birds and seaweeds. On rainy days, I had been reading a book at the trailer about edible seaweeds, one in particular called Dulse. "When fried in oil, tastes like potato chips." When the day's rain came, I harvested some Dulse and took it indoors to experiment. By then the men who had had the flat tire were back, so I made them some tea and got to work with the Dulse, some oil and salt, and an iron skillet. It was a noble experiment. But Dulse was barely edible. After the salt was licked off, it reminded me of chewing rubber bands. John said he liked it. Perhaps he was being polite; perhaps it reminded him of chewing tobacco. I recalled that on one walk we took together, John had pulled some sap off a tree and told me to chew it; he liked the flavor. I found it to be ghastly—the only natural product he offered me that I didn't like.

The next morning while John was checking the generator, I walked down to the beach. I saw coyote tracks in the sand, and lots of bird activity in the surf. The most spectacular sighting was of two golden eagles. They faced each other in the air, beak to beak, and twirled downward like a pinwheel. Later, John confirmed that he had seen that type of activity and had been told it was a mating ritual. But then, he added, it was too early in the year for that, so reckoned that they might have been two immature eagles playing at courting. That sounded reasonable to me.

That afternoon I caught another Dolly Varden after three casts. John said, "Well, I guess we can stop now." He cleaned the fish and with great expectations of seeing eagles, I took the guts, and my camera, down to the beach. John went off to repair the roof over the generator. I sat for an hour, waiting for spectacular footage. Nothing. Retreating to the trailer, I told John, "I tried to look like a rock." He replied, "Maybe you didn't hold your mouth the right way."

My task that evening was to untangle the fishing line that had become snarled while I was catching the Dolly Varden. So I wasn't perfect yet. After a good deal of advice, I worked and worked. After a half hour or so, I looked over at John and he was fast asleep in front of the TV, which he had tuned in to a program regarding abortion. A kind of panic sent upon me, since I knew he was much more conservative than I, so I ran off to the outhouse, thinking to escape a confrontation. It didn't work. He was awake when I returned, and asked my opinion. I took a deep breath, and bravely voiced my pro-choice opinion. To my surprise, he agreed. Once again, he demonstrated himself as a man of contradictions.

While John had worked shoveling gravel, he had noticed an interesting looking trail near the waterfall. The next day we set off to explore it, since a repair of the pump seemed hopeless. Walking in the woods there was quiet, with spongy moss underfoot. Sitka spruce limbs stood out nearly horizontal to the ground and were very close together. All the Devil's Club's large leaves slanted in the same direction. In the short time I had been at Dogfish Bay, the yellow daisies had gone to sleep; the lupine was gone; salmonberries were picked off or molded. The fireweed had changed from riotous blossom to pink fleshy stems. And it was cold. We walked for a while, until John "reckoned" that the Devil's Club was too thick for the clothes we had on. Its thorns scratched clear through our light-weight trousers. "We should have worn 'tin pants,'" John declared.

That's what he called dense rain gear. We retreated to the trailer for lunch.

I did find one pretty little purple flower called *geranium erianthum*. There was a book about wildflowers in the trailer that identified it for me after I had sketched it. The book advised, "Add Geranium leaves and flowers to your bath, and discover for yourself whether the herb is truly an aphrodisiac! Use sticky Geranium floral essence for freeing human potential!" I decided that sketching it would be enough for me. Besides, it would take bushels of it to remove that FRYMAX odor.

There were more visitors that day. A plane landed on the beach carrying an engineer and a contractor who wanted to look at the logging road. Over tea, John began talking to the engineer about the pump situation, so the contractor talked to me about the history of the Dogfish Bay operation. He said that about four years ago, natives had hired an attorney during land settlement activities. They had no money to pay him, so they gave him the timber rights. Then the attorney sold the timber rights to a Japanese company. In order for the operation to be a success, the company needed to cut 5 million board feet in a certain time period, but they cut only 1 million. So were trying to sell the company to a Korean company. Presumably the contract was being negotiated. The forest hadn't been clear cut, but still, I began to realize how beautiful old forests get destroyed. It seemed to me that the money seeking by Natives was out of character . . . at least a character I had always believed to be nobler than non-Natives. This gorgeous, wildlife-filled area had been scarred by a paved road and all this equipment lying about, not to mention the loss of selected trees. I was glad the business had failed. I wondered if the Natives were disappointed.

After the guests departed, John said he'd like to pick blueberries before the rain came. He was a great admirer of blueberries. He was always searching for the perfect ripeness, but rarely found it. When John was discussing blueberries with the Natives, he mildly rated the berries as not sweet enough. One Native replied, "You like them sweet? Put sugar on them." Our fingers were quickly stained, picking the plentiful fruit, and John's beard became so blue I called him "Bluebeard." We were surrounded by warblers flitting about. The area had not been completely ruined by timber companies.

The rain came. As we prepared our meal of trout and rice, we listened to weather reports on RATNET indicating a big storm was coming. John's expectations were confirmed by a telephone call from George that I might have to leave Dogfish Bay a day earlier than I expected. I was instructed to pack and be ready to leave on short notice. Although I was dismayed that I might have to leave early, I was reassured that bush pilots were smart enough to avoid flying in bad weather.

The next morning we had a leisurely breakfast because it was cold, overcast, and windy. Mid-morning the rain stopped sufficiently that we could walk.

Journal—August 13

We donned our "tin pants," as John calls rain gear, rubber boots and hats, and left to explore the old native trail that John had noticed behind the gravel pile by the waterfall. It was so cool— in both senses. Soft sphagnum moss and feather ferns underfoot. John finds trails by feeling for hard-packed ground under his feet. Devil's Club and ferns as high as our shoulders (thank goodness for the proper gear—we really would have been hurting without it). Sitka spruce all around, very close together. Squirrel middens, wonderful, thick, intricate moss growing on downed tree trunks. Blueberry bushes laden with fruit—even a few salmonberries. We came upon three native camps! One was a circle of rocks with a great fireplace. One with tree trunks leaned and tied at an angle so that a tarp could be thrown over to make a lean-to. The third had a ladder for some reason. The trail opened out on a modest bluff above the beach airstrip. John declared the camps were good for nothing—no water, bad for hunting.

It was so dark on the trail that most of my pictures did not turn out. I do have one shot of a can with holes in it. When I found it, I said, "Looks like someone was using it for target practice." John looked at it carefully and said, "Those are bear tooth holes. Look and see what was in the can. Bears'll tear apart anything for milk or cheese." Sure enough, the printing on the can said "American Processed Cheese." It was one of those squirt cans for putting cheese on crackers. John was right again!

He was also right about weather. When we returned to the trailer, George phoned again, and told me to prepare to leave. The storm was moving in. He'd be at Dogfish Bay by 4 or 5 o'clock.

And he was. George buzzed down on the beach. The little Cessna was buffeted by winds. Good-byes are hard, no matter if they're long and drawn out, or quick. John and I shared a quick hug. Tears came to my eyes. Then fright took over. It was nasty weather—25 mph winds, rain, and fog. We took off, shakily. George said, "I'm supposed to pick up a logger at Windy Bay, but a few minutes ago I couldn't land because of the winds. I'll try once more before I give up and just take you to Homer." It was a white-knuckle ride. On take-off, George called out, "Are you buckled up?" "Yes", I shouted. "Do you get air sick?" he yelled. "I never have . . . yet," I yelled back. I tried hard to seem calm. My right hand, which I hoped he couldn't see, was clenched in a death grip. I recalled all the reports I had read about bush pilots crashing. We bounced about. When he succeeded in landing in Windy Bay to pick up the logger, I could see that George was getting nervous as the wind blew the small craft from side to side. The logger wasted no time in jumping aboard behind me while throwing in a small bag. Within seconds we were off again. We passed unsteadily above a small island covered with Stellar Sea Lions. In a short time, we landed in Homer. Safe. We all smiled and breathed easier. The logger and I gave George heartfelt thanks.

Journal—August 13

How quickly surroundings have changed. This morning John and I arose around 7:30 for our usual breakfast and now, at 10:25 p.m., I'm here at a B & B overlooking Homer, watching the weather, but not in it.

The B & B was owned by friends of John. Well, who wasn't a friend of John's? It was a very pretty place, a bit away from town. George had driven me there, bless him. First on the agenda was a **shower.** Then I splurged on a cab to town for beer and a burrito.

The owners of the B & B were in the common room when I returned, sorting through blueberry leaves to dry and make into tea. I went to sleep. My fingers were still blue from previous berry picking, but my return to civilization was nearing completion. I had much to think about.

The next day, I browsed through books at the B&B, and copied down these quotes:

> Only my footsteps in the snow,
> Only the glow of my fire,
> Only a choir of wind to sing the benediction,
> But I feast on memories
>   In a holy place.
> It has been so long since I have heard my own
>   Voice,
> It startles me
> When I say the grace.
> May all things lost, apart, alone
> Find some small shelter of their own.
>   -from a Mountain Man's Christmas
>   By Bev Doolittle

> There are times . . . when one sits or walks in
> silence, overwhelmed by the glory of the
> moment.—Norman Lowell

> Light is the soul of the painting
> And without shadow
> There is no strength.—Norman Lowell

The next step back toward my everyday life took me by bus to Anchorage. The ride was pretty, though pouring rain. I wondered what John was doing; how he felt.

I visited the Anchorage Museum. An artist called Susie Silook had made a carving called "Mask of Post-Colonializational Trauma Tupilaks," with this caption: **"They sent in their missionaries and killed us with John 3:16."** That quotation haunts me wherever I go, from the United States, to Africa, to Australia, New Zealand, South America. What would be John's reaction to that?

There were flocks of white-haired men and blue-haired women wandering around Anchorage. Uh, oh, Princess Cruise people! They were clad in Reeboks and polyethylene windbreakers of lurid colors. At a gift store, one woman picked up a box labeled "Roadside Kill Pizza," and wondered why it was empty. They probably had only a few hours to "do" Anchorage and purchase souvenirs. I tried not to be smug, but did not succeed.

Journal—August 16

I've been close to grizzlies yet felt more fear as I walked by a drunken native man shouting and throwing a native woman to the pavement on the streets of Anchorage.

I took one last walk to Elderberry Park to say good-bye to Alaska. It was a lovely evening. There were many folks in the park, young people on roller-blades, joggers, cyclists, children playing, as well as tourists. Canada geese flew in to feed on the mud flats. The sky and mountains were an evening blue. I thought to myself, *"I am blessed."*

Cook Inlet
from Elderberry Park

In a matter of days, feeling rather schizophrenic, I returned to school to re-open my classroom and prepare lesson plans. Now I had had two different looks at Alaska, and both were much different from the Princess Cruise passengers whom I had seen roaming the edges of that great state. The question remained: how did I get so lucky to meet John and maintain this unique friendship? Was it just because I liked to write letters? Was it because I am a good listener? Surely I was not the only person he met whose habits did not irritate him. Maybe nobody else accepted his invitations! On his part, he had no expectations of me except friendship. I felt quite honored, since I knew he had plenty of Alaskan friends.

So the letters continued.

I sent him a poem:

> *One tree another tree*
> *Each standing alone and erect*
> *The wind and air*
> *Tell their distance apart*
> *But beneath the cover of earth*
> *Their roots reach out*
> *And at depths that cannot be seen*
> *The roots of the trees intertwine.*
> *—Spring 1940 by Ai Quing*

These words, I felt, described our friendship.

John related more trouble with the water system. He was also dismayed that the TV stopped working! That was a surprise to me. Apparently he had become used to television after so many years without. There was further trouble. It seems the English Bay Natives had stolen a propane tank from a supply shed. A TV tire tracks were seen by the shed. John's reaction to this also surprised me, for it was quite unforgiving. He declared he would not speak to the chief again and wrote one particularly long letter about how the Natives claimed to be converted to Russian Orthodoxy, and they should know about the commandments, and that if you break one commandment, you've broken them all, and maybe he would write to the archbishop in Anchorage. John was without his typewriter, and his handwriting seemed to be scrawled in anger. He summed up thus: *"Sometimes comes a storm."*

In another letter, he said that the logging company was putting him on their medical plan. *"I've discovered Government Health Insurance is valueless for me. I've had nothing but run-around from V.A., Vets Hospitalization, since they changed the rules. And Medicare is so . . . o . . . slow—no wonder some doctors won't accept Medicare patients. Therefore, I think Clinton's Health Insurance Plan (1993) would be just another bureaucratic mess."*

Perhaps John had been diagnosed with some illness, I thought.

He surely wasn't going to discuss it in detail with me. He made another curious comment: *"I would lie here and die before I'd LET the Natives help me. To help someone is a privilege. I would fight off unwanted help with my guns as long as I'd be able to at all."*

His only good news was that the water system seemed to be working. On October 15 (!) he *"planned to take a shower."* Whew!

In that same October letter, John told me that some men had visited him to help him winterize the camp, but they didn't stay till completion because they had to do their own winterizing at home.

He stated, *"I have lots to do before freeze up. And may snow soon. Guys brought a load of propane and buildings are now heated. Possible escape from cold for me if generators'd quit during cold temps, and I could find a place to keep spuds from freezing."* What a different scene from his cabin in the Talkeetnas, where he had just one small space to heat with his wood stove. He said winterizing was much less complicated there. And what a different scene it was in Florida, where, remarkably, we had had temperatures in the 50's for a few days; only a few days before the usual 80-degree weather returned.

Because of the theft, the Natives were then officially denied access to the camp. John declared he didn't miss them a bit. *"I like my privacy."* He added, *"Goat hunting begins this week end. English Bay Natives are allowing no hunters on 'their' land."* John had once stated that he didn't believe in "ownership" of land, but "prior use." Despite that, apparently he had little respect for nearby Natives. Was it because they had changed from their old ways and were becoming something different from their heritage? Why was he so angry? Was he glad I was gone from the camp, too?

And then, as if in answer to my wondering, he closed with, *"Nuff for now; think of you; hug, J."*

Despite his angry feelings for the Natives there, he continued to use the native name for Dogfish Bay. At the top of every letter was the date, followed by *Koyuktolik Bay*. And one sentence popped out: *"I despise inconsistency."*

On a whim, and because I knew that he had access to telephone, unlike anywhere else he had ever stayed, I phoned him one day. Afterwards, he wrote, *"Pleasant surprise, your phone call: we have become quite close friends."* Yes we had . . . on his terms, which was fine with me. When I imagined him visiting me in Florida, it just didn't compute. One night, I had a dream of him stepping off a plane in Fort Lauderdale, wearing his brown pants, plaid shirt and beaver hat, and going with me to an upscale restaurant. No, that would never work. I knew he had visited his cousin in Washington, once, but he was not a traveling man. I fit into his life pretty well, at least on a temporary basis, but I would never have left my job and friends to move north permanently. It remains one of my regrets, though, that I didn't get the opportunity to exchange teach for one year. It would have been interesting to see if I still loved Alaska as much in the long, dark winter.

By the end of October, John reported, *"sleeting all day here. Fella supposed to fly out and complete installation of new diesel generator, but weather has not permitted flying. He's supposed to bring a relief man for me so I could go into town (Homer). I'd like to be there on a Sunday so I could go trap shooting with my friends. And I should inquire of the old-timers in the Homer area if they know of a truck the Company could buy for here. We didn't own the pickup that was here, and now the owner wants it back. I'd need a truck for plowing snow."*

That set me to wondering how in the world they would get a truck there. I guess there was a road from somewhere, connecting with Homer, or maybe they'd bring it by boat? Turns out a barge was the answer.

The plow was needed to clear a place for a small plane to land. Other snow could be removed by shoveling.

Then, *"O, Company decided not to include me on their Blue Cross plan. Said at my age it'd disrupt too much. Rather, they'd plan to reimburse me directly. Well, I don't plan to lean on that much, anyway. I tend to doctor myself, stay away from M.D.s and clinics.*

Arthritis in writing hand is bothering me," he scrawled. *"I quit here."*

It wasn't easy for me to keep my letters interesting to him. I was sure he was not interested in hearing about details of my days teaching first grade, which took up most of my life. So I described my back yard birds, which were, and still are, quite plentiful in fall and winter. Painted buntings, blue-gray gnatcatchers, warblers of many kinds, come to my feeders, and I tried to interest him in that. He also heard about my canoe trips, where I saw ibis, herons, pileated woodpeckers, and wood storks. He seemed to like to hear about the birds, for, on a trip to town, he retrieved his bird book from storage and took it back to Dogfish Bay. We began exchanging reports of various bird sightings.

He did get to go trap shooting in Homer one Sunday during that autumn. *"I shot trap on Sunday, shot better than had been doing. I thought I might do better if 'got to Feeling better. We all shot well; couple new shooters, one a gal. I congratulated her. The Shooting is now hard for me: I must exert utmost effort/attention; 'used to be easy. But actually, in spite of failing Eyesight, failing Balance, ach-y Joints et al, I feel I am shooting better than ever before—both Shotgun and Rifle."*

Then he went into a long tirade against the Brady Bill, which he called *"a victory over National Rifle Ass'n."* Shades of my ex-husband! When I was newly married, my husband took me along on a trap shooting outing with my brand new father-in-law. No one in my family had ever owned a gun or went hunting. Of course I was trying to please my husband and acted eager to try, which I most definitely was not. It was so noisy! My shoulder hurt! But by golly, I actually hit one clay pigeon. I yelled "Yippee!" lowered the shotgun without removing my finger from the trigger, and nearly shot my foot off. That ended the history of Marge and guns. I thought to myself that it was probably a very good thing that John lived so far away.

The holidays approached. John wrote me on Thanksgiving Day. *"Been watching Macy's Thanksgiving Day Parade on TV."* (Good Grief!) *"Important to shovel Before walking on it—then freezes into ice and have to Chop it. Old 'woodsies' shovel First, Dudes walk on it. I'm no way blue about missing Thanksgiving festivities, nor Christmas, whatever. I consider it a sign of Maturity to have outgrown need for Holiday excitement. That also fits me for living here."*

"About 6 ½ hrs. 'Daylight' here now; still losing 4 ½ min/day. But that'll get less, not much more, since pretty close to Solstice. Sun disappears behind mts. To Southerly, doesn't show up til ca 10:30 a.m."

John wrote me a lot of letters during the dark winter.

"I've put up with a lot here; but worth it to Get Out of Town. People, as such, seem worth Zilch. I've recommenced to Philosophize; becomes apparent that's wrong with Humanity—for one—obsessed with Physical Gratification—not a big thing with me. Sometimes I feel I'm a century ahead—a Man of the Future."

My son was in Frankfort flying food to Bosnia. Janet, his wife, planned to fly to Germany to spend Christmas with him. It was to be the first Christmas since he was born that we would not be together. My mother and I muddled through, though not particularly joyously. Christmas is always a little weird in South Florida, if you have been reared in northern climates. Yes, I was used to wearing shorts on Christmas Day, but we always hope for a little cooler weather sometime in December, so we can light candles or even a fire in the fireplace. John reported seeing pure white hare and weasels romping about the camp. I wished I had been there to see them.

"Camp Manager asked if I wanted to go out for Christmas; I immediately replied NO as something might happen so I couldn't get back—like a lot of snow. I'd not be sad to be alone at Christmas. At Murder Lake one Christmas I had the whole area to myself; was a nice day, so I went and Cut some wood. I appreciate what happened the first Christmas, but I can do without the Tinsel and Feasting."

The Company must have been a bit worried about my friend John the recluse, so they arranged to fly in two friends of his from Homer, along with supplies for a traditional holiday dinner. Despite all his declarations that he did not like "festivities," he seemed quite pleased. He did remark that his guests couldn't understand why he liked remote living.

I had sent John a Christmas present of a wool sweater and socks. This was his reply: *By the way, thanks for your gifts via L.L.Bean. Beautiful Sweater—warm. And the Socks—I had plans to buy some and your gift Saved me a Step. Possibly you noticed when here how my socks had been extensively Darned* (yes, indeed) *anyway the gift was most appropriate and much appreciated. Somehow I'm not motivated to buy stuff for others at Christmas—I have no idea what they'd like. On the other hand, if I'd see someone needing something I had, I'd give it to them, even like on July 4. I guess my way is another expression of my non-conventionalism."*

But Happy New Year! John seemed to have all equipment working in the trailer for the winter.

Ours was a strange friendship. As gentlemanly as John was toward me and his acquaintances, he wrote of a side to him I had not seen.

"I feel I have Nothing worthy of your admiration—unless one'd count Honesty as a virtue. I would be Gentle, in so far as possible, but as if someone'd display a Bad Attitude, I get ideas like they should be Eliminated (Permanently). I realize that is not a nice, attitude on my part—not conventionally accepted. So, it's good I'm here, where I am.

"This job—is nearest thing to Heaven I've experienced in my life: Fish, Berries, Great Air and Water; no expenses—I can save 20 thou/year. So what would I do with all the money? I could travel, but no place I want to go. I'm thinking about some philanthropical projects. I could buy a fancy new Car, but I don't want one . . . ? I don't like to Drive, and no place I'd want to go where a road'd take me."

Disturbing words to hear . . . but, again, why would I have shown a bad attitude to this man when we were the only two in the wilderness? It's amazing to me now that I was not alarmed enough to ease off on the friendship. I did write back and ask him what was his definition of "a bad attitude." I can remember that I was rather relieved that he didn't want to travel. Now no more worries about how we would ever get along in South Florida. But why was the job on Dogfish Bay "the nearest thing to Heaven" he had experienced in his life? What about all those years at Murder Lake? I sent him some pictures of the painted buntings that visited my back yard each winter. Perhaps a spot of color would cheer him up.

Aha! I received an answer to my question! *"Yes, you did well to question my definition of 'bad attitude.' My idea of that is people who strive to satisfy, gratify, what they want, with no regard for effects of that pursuit on any/all other people. When this is carried far enough, and they are caught, prisons are full of them, where they reside at the expense of those they were 'ripping off.'"* However, he offered no easy answer about carrying out the "elimination" of the folks with a bad attitude.

Early that year (1994) some friends in England wrote and invited me to join them for a trip to Tuscany, where they have a place.

I was thrilled, and accepted their invitation. John had been hinting at another visit to Alaska, so I wrote: *"I don't want you to become burdened with me as a yearly visitor. It's very tricky, isn't it, to enjoy visits and not have them become obligations. We'll play it by ear. I'm counting on you to be honest and let me know if you really want me to visit again or if you're happier on your own."* Who wouldn't wonder, after his frequent comments? I was playing it safe. I really couldn't refuse the invitation to Tuscany! We would be driving from my friends' home in Bedfordshire. Another new experience! At the same time, I certainly didn't want to hurt John's feelings.

He responded: *"Sure. I'd think it fine if you visited me here again, but, like you wrote, who knows for sure what will be going on with me, or at least this place, by next summer. I hope to stay here—I despise the Town Scene.* (He could have fooled me! He had been so gracious and active in Homer, and everyone seemed to like him.)

That spring my mother and I drove to Fayetteville, N.C., to visit my son and his wife. I hadn't seen him in over a year. We tromped around looking at birds and went canoeing. My letters to John afterward were easy to write, as I described the birds I had seen. Red-cockaded woodpeckers! Cedar waxwings! Wood ducks! All new and exciting to me. John responded by saying how he had enjoyed birding at Murder Lake: *The Yellow-rumped Warbler was one of the first returning migrants to Murder Lake in Spring; along with Slate-colored Junco; and of course the ducks. I had a great time spotting birds there and it was noted by ornithologists as the richest place in a large area around for variety and number of bird species. I identified ca. 115 species within 2 miles of the cabin while there.*

He wrote of having money to spend on extravagances (for him) like a bow made to his design. It would kill a moose! "Oh, no," I thought. More weapons. My ex-husband liked bows and arrows, too. At least they are not noisy. He bought me a beautiful double curve bow and encouraged me to take archery lessons while I was in college. My experience with that sport was not much more impressive than my shotgun skills. I shot my sorority pin right off my left breast in one lesson. John also had ordered a shotgun made according to his design, from Italy!

March, 1994—John wrote that he was *"now in 81st year."* And still shooting accurately though he couldn't identify a bird without binoculars. At one point he remarked, *"the birds don't care what you call them."* His letters from Dogfish Bay were terrible scrawls—he hadn't taken his ancient Underwood typewriter with him. He hated ball point pens. The only time he wrote a swear word was in relation to a pen.

Winter was hanging on that year. There was more trouble with the generator and a resulting frozen water system. But John tolerated it all and tried his best to fix things whenever possible. When it was too dreary or icy to go outside, he took to working crossword puzzles. He had found a book of them in the trailer. His letters sometimes became angry tirades about politicians and damage to the environment. (I wished he would stick to birds.) Then this ominous sentence: *"After this job I'd be Homeless."*

"Recemt developments (Company) could mean my job might be nearing its ending here. So I'm uncertain about inviting company during Summer. Meanwhile, I'm thinking about Alternate Landing Sites. I've tried phoning Seldovia Seniors—no answer. Plane to Homer 6 days hence. I'd find out from Senior Center there. I feel I don't want to return to Homer to stay. Too much of the discordant Human Element, I'm intolerant of 'bustling people.' All I want to do is Get Away from them. If they'd crowd me past the breaking point, I could go berserk. So best I remain apart."

He wrote that after telling me how kind and inclusive one family had been in Homer, and how he valued their friendship, and mine. It was puzzling, to say the least. I wrote back about a canoe trip I had made, and . . . . birds!

I kept rough drafts of all the letters I wrote to John in those days, as well as all of his letters. Why wasn't I more disapproving of what he said? For example, he wrote that he had been reading Carl Sagan: *"Fairly heavy reading. He seems a convinced Darwinist. I am not. I do not contest that there were more primitive humanoids on Earth before, but I do not think we are descended from them."* Did I write back and express my astonishment that he didn't believe the science of Darwin? No. So when I read my thoughts in my journals about how inconsistent he was, I have to admit I was just as inconsistent, or at least less than truthful, about my beliefs. It wouldn't have been dangerous to oppose his viewpoints by mail, for goodness sake. I guess I was still angling for another invitation to experience wilderness. What kind of a friend was I, to hide my beliefs? A "phony" one, to use one of John's favorite words. In my mind, what bound us in friendship was our appreciation and respect of wilderness, and that outweighed our differences. Especially since we actually saw each other so infrequently.

In April, John wrote that he had looked at a place to stay in Seldovia. It looked agreeable. *"I got along well with (the) Manager, who is a Baptist preacher. (Yikes! was my agnostic reaction.) Looks like I'll be outta here (Dogfish Bay) by June 1. The Deal is Made, the Corporation is giving it up, and I plan to leave, tho I was asked to stay on by President of English Bay Native Corporation. I declined.*

I figure an Intelligent person may foresee a bad situation and avoid it . . ."

As John planned his move to Seldovia, I planned a trip to England. My mother, at age 83, dearly wanted to attend a cousin's wedding in Cornwall, and she didn't want to go alone. She purchased my ticket, and I gladly accepted. The whole family was going to stay in a farm B & B: Mom and I; two brothers and three sisters of the bride-to-be, and assorted offspring of the cousins, one of whom was to be christened the day after the wedding, in the same 500-year-old village church. I purchased a flowered dress and a big hat for the occasion and off we went. That trip is a whole other story, and it's a good one.

I returned home with a nasty cold; finished up my end-of-the-year classroom duties, and prepared to return to England to meet up with my friends in Bedfordshire for our trip to Tuscany. I promised John I'd send him postcards. It's clear that when I received an invitation, I rarely turned it down! More good adventure, albeit highly civilized.

On my return, I wrote one of my better letters, which I quote here:

Dear John, Your letter of June 29 was here when I returned home last Thursday. Thanks. It's taken me a few days to shift gears back into the home "mode." It was a wonderful trip, full of medieval architectural wonders, but I grew homesick for—of all things— American accents, so I'm happy to be back. There are many things to attend to here. I've had an infestation of carpenter ants in my kitchen, dental work and medical appointments I like to take care of when I'm not working.

My British friends and I drove this route: London to Dover; ferry to Calais; to Paris, Nice, Tuscany (Sienna, Florence, Venice) Austria, Metz, Calais again, and back to London. We stayed a week in Tuscany, in the country, so it wasn't all city touring. As my friends said, we drove down the Rhone and up the Rhine.

Having never been to the continent before, I was intrigued by the old walled cities and awe-struck by the large cathedrals; by the engineering feats done so long ago, and by the sheer amount of man hours and artistic skills devoted to the church. It's different from being awe-struck by the natural wonders of Alaskan wilderness.

I feel that many Europeans treat nature as something to conquer and keep separate from rather than something of which we are a part. My British friends teased me for my environmental concerns, and chide me for not having more interest in people. I asked them what issue more directly affects people than the environment!

Saw many art treasures in the Louvre and the Uffizi. My best times were in the small villages on hillsides stitched all around by vineyards, and on my solitary walks around Tuscany, where I enjoyed the wildflowers and huge fields of sunflowers.

My limited abilities in French and Italian were useful and I found the people friendly and charming.

The Alps in Austria were majestic, but everywhere, those huge, power line stantions! Quite too much civilization to be as lovely as Alaska.

I feel very lucky to have had the opportunity to go with my friends on this venture, for I am curious about this old world.

John, also, was now in a place slightly more civilized than Dogfish Bay. Seldovia isn't exactly a booming metropolis. His new address was "General Delivery, Seldovia, Alaska." He reckoned that it was a good thing we hadn't planned to meet that year. He scheduled a cataract operation.

The first letter I received from Seldovia was typed on onion skin (remember that?) *"Broke my old Typer out of Storage; Ribon dried up; none available here . . ."* He wasn't kidding. It was like trying to read rapidly drying invisible ink. And even then, in 1994, I wondered who still sold typewriter ribbons for an old Underwood.

He noted *"I can be as miserable here as any place else; so why not stay where I am?"*

Why he was miserable he did not say . . . away from the wilderness? I wrote back: *I am sad that you are miserable. You told me once that you have been blessed by the gift of faith. I believe I have been blessed, and grateful for, small gifts—the song of a bird, the sight of a flower, the smile of a friend, a cold drink of water. Maybe I am just simple-minded!"* My, I was getting brave! Was I trying to scold him?

He returned *"Yes, I regret to have to say that it's been a long time since I've Felt Good. But I stumble along, by way of working out God's Plan for my life. I also enjoy bird songs, pretty/aromatic Flowers—and I can stare with admiration at artistic arrangements in the Skies."*

That was interesting to me. Since the only times I had ever been in Alaska, night did not fall until bed time, and I had never seen stars in the Northern skies. I guessed that in the winter, skies must be misted and gray. But what did I know? I have seen glorious skies in the Dry Tortugas and Patagonia, in the absence of ambient light, but my clearest night-time memory of skies in Alaska was a full moon rising at 11 p.m. That was special. I should have asked if he was talking about clouds!

John had taken to ending his letters with *"bye for now, Soul Mate."* I felt like a hypocrite. Memories of John and his life were becoming self-analysis.

The cataract surgery had gone well, and he was target-shooting better than ever, so he said. The next step for John was acquiring a Post Office Box, the cost of which was $7.25 per year. He was advised that P.O. Boxes are used by "pillars of the community," while General Delivery was for the flotsam and jetsam. So my next letter began with *"Dear Pillar of the Community . . ."*

Then, in September came a letter from Homer, scrawled in pencil on yellow legal paper. John was sick. *"This illness is a major segment of my life. My most gracious hosts couldn't see me returning a week ago in the shape I was in.* I struggled to read the scrawl. *"My doc says if it's internal cancer, You Don't Get Better . . . I've blessed you for the lamb's wool sweater, which I have been wearing sometimes day and night. I have zero energy."* He gave up his 62-year habit of chewing tobacco and said the imported beer he used to enjoy no longer tasted good. It was a pitiful letter from such a self-reliant person. He said he didn't have enough hand control to do leatherwork.

Then, 10 days later, he returned to Seldovia, weak but feeling better, at least well enough to look after himself. But he said he felt no joy in life now, nor could he foresee any joy in the future. He tended to be "irascible." I felt helpless to offer any comfort. How lucky he was to have the friends in Homer. I had met them after my stay at Murder Lake. They were the ones who owned an antique shop in Homer and were long-time fans of his. They sold his leatherwork from their store.

Gradually, John regained his health, though from that point on, his letters did reveal increasing "irascibility." *"I see no brightness in the future. Only human idiocy, heaped on more human idiocy. I get that way sometimes. I seem to have enough Irish that when turned off, Nothing can please me. I hope this is not too depressing to you. I've gone thru these 'downs' before, got over it. Guess I keep it sufficiently covered so people don't seem to notice."*

Despite the gloom, he resumed his leatherworking and trap shooting. He resolved to find better hearing aids. However, as time passed, he became more and more discontented with his apartment and his church in Seldovia.

Meanwhile, my son had been sent to Saudi Arabia with the Air Force. My mother and I went to North Carolina to visit my daughter-in-law. Directly after that, my mother became quite ill and required my full-time attention. To add to the stress and confusion,

Hurricane Gordon passed near my area with rain and flooding, but the winds were not strong enough to close the schools. There was a lapse in my letter-writing.

Spring arrived. I began to think about summer travel. Very tentatively, I wrote, *"Am trying to think ahead and plan some kind of 'retreat' for this summer. Would appreciate your thoughts. It sounds as though where you are staying might not be such a good place for me to visit . . . also don't know your exact health/mood/inclination. But if you would like some company, I always enjoy visiting you. There's also the question of my mother's health. It's problematic, for one day she's perfectly fine, then another day she wakes up on the floor and doesn't remember fainting.* (She was 85 years old at that time.)

He answered that he couldn't recommend my visiting Seldovia. There wasn't *"much to do. Besides, I'm not in a mood to be good company. It's a good thing Earth is not flat as ancients believed, with an edge to jump off."*

I wasn't surprised. The closest I came to offering advice was to suggest listening to music, and to quote W. H. Auden:

> "the funniest mortals and the kindest are those who are
> most aware of the baffle of being, don't kid themselves
> our care is consolable, but believe a laugh is less heartless
> than tears."

I got no response from John on the quote, but he did start listening to music! Soon I was writing to him complaining about my woes. My mother was very ill again; my house had to be tented because of termites; shortly after that my house was burglarized. I got away when I could, canoeing and birding. The grand finale for that summer was Hurricane Erin, which came close enough to Fort Lauderdale to require shuttering up my house, a huge job for me because the aluminum panels were so heavy and awkward.

John began looking for another place to live. Perhaps Dillingham, he thought, or Haines. He applied for senior housing in

Haines, but didn't receive a reply from them. He visited Homer quite a few times. I wondered why he just didn't move back there, but he said he wouldn't consider it. His reason? *"There's too much of The Other Element, I can't stand. 'Times I feel there's No Place On Earth for me."* I wrote back that a 72-year-old friend of mine, also named John, who had been my Audubon canoeing companion for years, had undergone knee replacement surgery. His view? "Staying healthy is just dying real slow."

Christmas (1995) came and went. My son brought me frankincense from Saudi Arabia. John reported going for medical tests in Anchorage. The doctor's concern, "which cost me money," was cancer, and he had been given a program of treatment which was supposed to "mitigate symptoms common in aging males."

Every author John read was male. I couldn't resist quoting Pat Conroy: "There is a mountain range between the sexes with no exotic race of Sherpas to translate the enigmas of those deadly slopes that separate us." And in reply to that, John said, *"I have been helped with a problem a number of times by women; they could see an angle to which I seemed blinded. I think this may be an important reason God made us different; a couple, working together, thus can achieve a more complete outlook, perhaps than either could attain alone."*

March, 1996, was not a pleasant one for me, and included a bout with bronchitis and trouble with my boss. He asked for a "personal favor" by supporting his petition to waive certain policies set by the School Board. I declined to sign the petition and the situation escalated. I am proud to say that one teacher called me the "Rosa Parks of the school" for speaking up when others were afraid. It became clear to me that a transfer to another school would be in my best interest. So I contacted a man I had previously worked for. He was happy to welcome me back and arranged the transfer for me to his school. During the turmoil, I took to reading Ambrose Bierce, and quoted him in my letters to John.

> *Politics: a strife of interests masquerading as a contest of principles.*

> *Conservative: a statesman who is enamored of existing evils, as distinguished from the Liberal, who wishes to replace them with others.*

Then—in May—big news. Finally, approval came from housing in Haines that John had been accepted. He seemed delighted.

A letter arrived from a post office box in Haines, postmarked July 10, 1996. (Postage: 32 cents. I noted that the first letter I had received from him in 1991 had a stamp worth 29 cents.) "*So here I am at Haines. My application for housing surfaced. I drove the 1000* *miles from Homer; stopped overnight at Anchorage—stayed with friend—to meet Dr.'s appointment. Tests that Specialist wanted. Blood test revealed I'm anemic. I think that must be from the injections prescribed to alleviate prostate problem. I'm considering stopping that treatment—injections last three months, cost ca. $1000; Medicare pays most of it.* And additionally, a whopper of a statement: *"I'd become somewhat hung-up on a lady friend at Seldovia, whom I'd helped fix up a number of items not functioning at her place: ridiculous at my age.*

I hope to retain her as a friend. Otherwise the feeling about her will fade with time, and best so." No wonder he didn't want me to visit Seldovia! But of course I had not written of any male interests I had in Florida, either. So we were even! I had two selves, as well, or maybe more. One of my all-time favorite poems is "Plaint of Complexity" by Eunice Tietjins. It starts out "I have too many selves to know the one . . . ."

That summer I had bladder surgery. What the docs called "minor surgery" was not so minor to me. John said we were both "guinea pigs" for the medicos. He taped a four-leaf clover to his letter and prayed God would guide me to what was best for me. One or the other worked. I recovered and went off to visit my son and his wife in North Carolina; I also looked at my land and attempted, unsuccessfully, to begin building on my lot. It proved too complicated—something that I could not do in steps: Couldn't dig a well until I knew where the cabin would go; couldn't decide where the cabin would go until I knew where the driveway would go, etc. The tasks seemed overwhelming and too costly. It was frustrating. NO MAN TO HELP ME!!!! When I wrote of my difficulties, John replied, *"Well, I don't know when we'd meet again; I couldn't do you much good at present state and time. Don't let 'em horswoggle you on work at N.C. property."* Story of my life—bad timing!

About the time John finally wrote the words "prostate cancer" and said that a blood test was "not good," I was selected to sit on a jury. (Talk about a whole other story!) This was such a long and arduous experience (three weeks, homicide), our correspondence suffered as well.

By fall, both of us were feeling well. John, especially, seemed rather frisky, writing about his female friend from Seldovia and . . . a new one in Haines! He said he did not seek them out, they came to him. Of one, he declared, "This is an admirable woman, and 'seems to have some regard for me." He actually visited the lower 48 that fall . . . . his cousin in Sequim. He was also pleased that a publisher in Haines was interested in publishing his book, "The Friendly Wilderness," with both his words and illustrations. He adopted a cat and named it Put-ankhamon. He began teaching someone (female) leatherwork. He received his leather by mail. The following paragraph illustrates how differently John lived:

*I phoned in the order. First time ever talked with the Tannery. I'd always written before. They have "800" number. I used a neighboring tenant's phone. I haven't had a phone for 41 years (*He forgot about the one at Dogfish Bay). *Little bills I don't have to pay. I don't have a TV either. Here it costs $30/mo for TV, $40 to get the "good" station. At the $30 rate one gets to watch the commercials; one pays for power to watch something one doesn't want. Somehow I'm opposed to that scene. Besides, basically, I'm against paying for amusement; I feel I should be able to find sufficient amusement without incurring expense, or using up non-renewable natural resources. I have radio and a hoard of good music on cassettes. I did feel required to subscribe to the small "weekly bleat" paper, nearly $40/yr.; but split that with a neighboring tenant here. It's the only way here to learn what's ongoing in this community. At Seldovia, was no paper—'d been tried but failed. News was posted on Bulletin Boards, at the General Store and at the Post Office. It worked entirely well.*

That winter, my son was discharged from his obligations to the Air Force, he and his wife sold their little house in Fayetteville, and they set off for a year of travel. What a fine adventure! I admired their planning and bravery. The trip took them from Amsterdam to Germany, South Africa, Zimbabwe, Nairobi, the Seychelles,

Singapore, Malaysia, Thailand, Bangkok, Bali, Java, Australia, New Zealand, Fiji Islands, Hawaii, and back to the USA.

So 1997 arrived.

Mail service to Haines was sporadic since it all came by plane from Juneau, where, according to John, flying weather in winter was notoriously bad. John reckoned that *"Mail situation here should help in cultivation of Patience."*

The winter blues seemed to have taken over John's life. *"Tho here only 6 months, already seeds of discontent being here are germinating. Already I'm looking for another area. I wrote about applying for Watchman/Caretaker at a site owned by Nature Conservancy—as you prob'ly know, places they purchase to preserve habitat. I know the lady who was Alaska Director for N.C. For some such job I'd be out of here. Perhaps my Last Stand."*

I, on the other hand, was excited about being the campaign treasurer for my good friend Tim, who was running for City Commissioner. It was new for me to be involved in city politics, and I liked it.

John's January letter read, *"By radio I hear that this is an especially severe winter in some other parts of Alaska; like 30 below zero F. at Anchorage, and a woman found dead at Fairbanks, demise attributed to cold. Said 'last severe Winter was '88/'89— that was the year I moved to Homer, so I didn't notice it. Between suspected Anemia, still, and Old Age, I seem to have lost a lot of former ability to withstand Cold. Reasons for my staying in Alaska are becoming less: I don't Hunt any more, no place to Flyfish except by a long trip; only the Longevity Bonus and Permanent Fund Dividend—ca. $4000 annually, I'd lose it if I left. I have "Feelers out for two different remote-site positions . . ."*

In March, John's book arrived, nicely inscribed:

To Marge;
    Friend, Consultant
       And Faithful Correspondent.
        John Ireland

I treasured it.

My letter of March 16 thanked him for the book and asked for the address of the store selling them. I wanted to order more copies for my school library and my friends.

I went on to say, *"Last weekend was a superior one in every way. I took Friday off and went up near Gainesville for a canoeing weekend. I got the chance to drive up with the outfitter (named John) who is always interesting, and since it was such a long drive (6 hours) he brought along some tapes of Bill Moyers interviewing Joseph Campbell on mythology. I found the conversations thought-provoking. The weather was perfect, dogwoods blooming, also azaleas; warblers everywhere. I was quite comfortable in my tent for two nights. The first day we paddled the Santa Fe; the second, the Ichetucknee (both tributaries of the Suwanee). These rivers are wonderful and clear, with frequent natural springs bubbling along the way. For the most part, we (our party of eight) were the only folks on the rivers save the wildlife. A barred owl watched us early one morning, staring and turning its head from side to side. As the bow of our canoe passed under, he flew to cover, soundlessly as a ghost."*

That spring was magical in another way . . . . my neighbor won the election to City Commissioner. It was quite a coup for the common person! His win over a former State Speaker of the House was a true grass-roots accomplishment.

To complete the satisfactory quality of that spring, there came an invitation from Haines, although a rather half-hearted one:

What are your plans for 'coming summer? If I'd survive, I plan to be here during July, if you'd want to come and spend some time. I'd consider there's not a great deal to hold one's interest for an extended time at this place. I have been more bored, and even at times a bit lonely, at this place, than at any time or place during my entire life. I feel the feelings of loneliness are an aspect of elder years; and being bored is, I'd say always and entirely one's own fault.

It didn't take me long to accept the invitation, and since he wasn't anticipating an "extended" stay, I began to plan a trip that would involve more stops than Haines. Looking back at the plans, I am amazed, once again, at how adventurous I was. My solo trip took shape. While reading the Mileposter (the ultimate independent traveler's guide to Alaska), I "took a notion" to visit a native settlement. I picked Angoon, an island on the ferry route to Haines, where one was most likely to see bears. In addition, a train trip out of Haines to Skagway seemed like fun. I offered to pay John's way if he should be so inclined to join me. Since all my plans seemed to be agreeable with John, I added one more side trip after I planned to leave Haines: a boat trip up Tracy Arm Fiord. I wrote: *No meetings! No telephone! No little kids*!

Then, out of nowhere, I learned another side to my pal John:

May 17, 1997: *Yesterday I was a judge at a large State-wide, home brewing competition. This is more of a chore than pleasure, as some products entered are less than pleasant in taste. Were about 35 judges, small groups assigned to different types of brew. In return for our time/effort expended, judges receive free passes to 'beer tasting' and barbeque this afternoon. Otherwise $25. This, I understand, is sampling different commercial brews, some of which might be quite good. As I am rated as something of an expert on brews of the traditional variety, it is 'in keeping' that I become acquainted with some commercial brews I've never tried. I had not arrived here at this time last year when this was ongoing; but understand it's the best party of the year.*

How little we knew each other.

9

Day of departure arrived: July 7, 1997—Another adventure.

I stayed at Douglas Island, outside Juneau. Lovely B&B with a basket by the door for shoes. No shoes inside—everyone could choose a pair of slippers. Mud is ever present in Alaska. I settled in.

Next morning, I was determined to hike a trail that I had some difficulty finding.

Journal—July 8

Finally found a woman who directed me to trail. Sweating quarts by this time, and backpack too heavy. I should forget my zoom lens unless in car. Period. Up, up. Should have had water. One more thing to carry. Banana snatched from breakfast would have gone bad. Alas. Identified Varied Thrush, also Chestnut-backed Chickadees. Cheerful lot. Heard a woodpecker—didn't see it. Pine Siskins. A hummer buzzed past. Creaked back. Saw Steller's Jay and a big fat robin.

Then I sat on the porch and watched hummingbirds at the feeders before I took off for supper. I had a great halibut dinner with two glasses of extremely pleasant Cabernet Blanc.

The next day I "rented a wreck." The Grand Am had a dandy horizontal crack clear across the windshield. I purchased $15 worth of gas ($1.43/gallon—this IS history) and roared off to Mendenhall Glacier. After dodging several dozen tourists, I pretty much had the place to myself. Arctic terns hovered and swooped, herring gulls floated about on chunks of ice, and enormous mosquitoes buzzed around me. On the Moraine Ecology Trail, I saw Wilson's Warblers, Hermit Thrush, Yellow and Orange-Crowned Warblers, and had a spectacular look at the Glacier, sans hordes. I got excited to see a dark-headed bird on the ground, then remembered what my son once told me: "Just when you think you've found something good, it's only a dark-eyed Junco." Fooled again.

When it began to rain, I jumped in the car and drove to a mall. It was called the Nutmeg Mall. I bought some postcards and stamps. It seemed exotic that I wrote a card to my son and daughter-in-law in Fiji (they had listed several General Delivery options to keep in touch during their world tour). How much farther away could we get from each other?

Leaving the mall, I proceeded to get confused in hilly downtown Juneau. It was no small accomplishment for me to parallel park on a hill. Juneau was crowded with tourists but there were irresistible shops. The whale bone spirit mask I purchased that day still hangs over my fireplace.

The following morning I had arranged to catch the LeConte Ferry at (gasp) 3 a.m. The car rental folks had told me to leave the car at the ferry dock (which was quite a distance from town) lock the doors, throw the keys into the truck, and close it. They'd find it and open it up with their spare keys. This maneuver took some deliberate thinking on my part. I was terrified I'd leave something inside the car. And I did have some nagging doubts about "catching" a cab on my return to this rather remote docking location. But all went well, and soon I was aboard the boat, cozy, with adventure right outside the window.

After a three-hour nap, a muffin and two cups of coffee, I woke at 7 a.m. as the ferry stopped at Hoonah. At least a dozen eagles were fishing. Harbor Porpoises swam about. Back underway, at 10 a.m., the captain announced "Whale! Near shore, port side! Humpback!"

An hour later, we docked at Angoon. I had seen an ad for a B & B in the Mile Poster, and had made a reservation. A Native man named Harold was to meet me at the dock. And there he was. Harold was slightly built, with brown hairless hands, short, stiff, salt and pepper hair, sparse beard and moustache, fine white teeth, and a broad smile. He had a habit of rubbing his eyes and his stiff hair as if he were just waking up. He took me to the B & B and said he would pick me up at 1:00, and for $7 would give me a tour of the island so I would know where everything was located.

Journal:

This place is NEW—log cabin . . . a sign facing the road says 'open' in NEON making it an interesting combination of pleasant and jarring. Cabin beautifully made, and sits on the only road in Angoon. Traffic hard to figure in a place this small. Naturally the only way I can get anywhere is on foot . . . along the road, which Harold told me proudly, was paved just last summer. 'Makes it a lot easier on our cars," he said. His is an Isuzu station wagon. Harold keeps asking me why I came to Angoon. At this point I'm wondering, too.

Dodging traffic, I did see a hermit thrush and some golden crowned kinglets. I heard high st-st-st many times before catching two with my binocular. They were high in a spruce. One Junco; ravens, crows, and eagles. Harold told me the main tribes here are Ravens and Eagles; moieties (descent groups) of the Tlingit People.

Well as to the tour, the island was depressing—tumbles of subsidized housing mixed in with decaying tribal houses, two schools (grammar and high), one convenience store, one market (Angoon Trading Post), one café (Ramona's) and one gas station. Harold used to be the custodian at one of the schools. Litter lined the road. There were many Bud cans, though the town is "dry."

We went to the dump (not landfill or transfer/recycling station) to see bears, but all we saw was smoking trash.

There was a float plane dock. Happy news was that I found salmonberries along the ditch adjacent to the road.

After Harold dropped me off at the B & B, I trotted down to the Trading Post and bought cheese and crackers for my supper.

Journal:

These folks seem unaware of the treasures around them. Harold said, 'There aren't many birds around here, just eagles and ravens.'. Trees are chopped down and lay around. I saw a native girl with green nail polish. Kids ride dirt bikes and swoop around on roller blades. Here, the cabin has TV, answering machine, and microwave. People are people, I guess. All wanting the 'in' things. Political posters were plastered on the village houses.

Here's the clincher: I'm the ONLY person in this huge 4-bedroom place. The owners don't stay here. Breakfast food is in the refrigerator. Harold went home, but before leaving, he told me if I heard dogs barking, I shouldn't go out, because that meant there were bears in the yard.

I bundled up and sat on the porch to draw, listening to hummingbirds zoom by, then inside to read. What a strange night.

Next day was even stranger. I examined my options for breakfast. Harold had told me that he couldn't get any milk in Angoon ("Sometimes they have it; sometimes they don't.") so he left some milk that had been frozen previously. I settled on oatmeal, and had just started to read when in came Harold. Four cups of coffee and a long conversation later . . .

First the conversation: Harold, though Native, was a Republican, pro-oil, and non-conservationist. He had four children, one of whom was schizophrenic and had "snapped." She was then in Sitka "hearing voices." Another daughter was in Juneau and was a speech therapist. Harold's reckoning was "Natives don't want to see Natives get ahead." There was a tackle shop attached to the B & B, and Harold was running it. "But," he said, "Natives won't patronize it now, though they used to when White folks owned it." He said the Native Council usually elects a White mayor. Most of the teachers and all of the preachers (Russian Orthodox, Assembly of God, Presbyterian and Salvation Army) were White.

"My people," said Harold, "were purse seiners." (A purse seine is a large net designed to be set by two boats around a school of fish and so arranged that after the ends have been brought together the bottom could be closed.) Harold and his wife (where was she? I wondered) had fought for a land grant. Natives got timber rights, mineral rights, and fishing rights. Harold's brother had sold his fishing permit for $40,000. He opined that the Japanese were taking control of the fish industry. "My people were fishermen. Take that away and what do you have left?" Harold complained.

Hmm, I wanted to experience a Native village, and I did. It was not at all what I expected. I had assigned certain purity to Natives that was apparently long-gone, I was sad to admit.

I had to get out of the cabin, so I strolled outside. At the Angoon Market, I heard a voice on the radio warning that "deep kissing can spread AIDS, especially if your gums bleed." I bought a candy bar. As I passed the dump, I noticed it was still smoking. Harold had told me they "have to burn every day." Just as I sat down on a 4 x 4 at the float plane dock, the rain came, so I hoofed it back to Sophie's. Harold was watching a movie called Foreign Body, laughing loudly. When I retired to my room at 1:25 p.m., I wrote: "God, I hope it doesn't rain all day."

At 5:30, p.m., I wrote, "It did. Still is."

Harold talked to me all afternoon.

A citizen' band radio played all day, in the background. Messages were varied: "Judy, come home now." "The mess is cleaned from the dump now so it's safe to drive in without getting a flat." "Please dump where you're supposed to dump." After Harold heard that last message, he muttered, "That was the Mayor . . . . limited learning." Other messages stated, "Bob, come get our garbage. The bears just knocked it all over the yard." And "K-bl-bl (2-year-old babble) Suzie, get off the radio!" Last, "Apply for job by 2 p.m."

An Alaska Geographic magazine (Vo. 1, No. 3, Summer, 1973), was in the common area in the cabin. There was an article about Admiralty Island. "As the people became established on the land, they slowly developed a culture elaborately intertwined with the creatures that influenced their daily lives. The Tlingit Nation evolved into two cultural divisions, one became Eagle . . . . the other became Raven . . . . other animals, beaver, killer whale, frog, bear, were classes within the two divisions."

This is essentially what Harold told me. He is Eagle (sub-tribe Wolf) and his wife, Raven (sub-tribe Dog-salmon). He knew a few phrases in Tlingit, but he was not allowed to speak it in school. Neither was he allowed to keep his Native name. Native crafts were no longer produced on Angoon.

Late that afternoon I headed out, somewhat desperately, toward Ramona's, wearing wellies and rain parka.

Ramona's was a big room with mismatched tables and chairs, a microwave, and several food cases—some working, some not. A partially worked jigsaw puzzle occupied one table. There were photographs of various berries on the wall. A candy case was prominent. Candy seemed to be a popular item in Angoon. Ramona said to me, "Why are you in Angoon?" Again, I wondered why, indeed. I said, "To see bears."

My dinner consisted of a pepperoni pizza pocket sandwich (which was microwaved), a cup of herbal tea, and a cookie. Quite a few young folks came in to buy candy while I was eating.

Afterwards, I walked around "town." Totems were animal shapes mounted on poles. I was disheartened at the enormous amount of trash everywhere. The beach was totally disgusting— even two wrecked bikes were on the sand. Houses were surrounded by paper plates, and just plain junk. The houses were in disrepair, and some still had Christmas lights up. I thought "birds don't mess their own nests."

When I returned to my lodging, it was pouring. I remembered what Harold had said frequently: "Lotta rain, eh?"

The following morning I woke to dripping from the roof, but not steady rain. I was determined to spend the day outdoors, rain or not. After a minimal breakfast, I donned two pairs of socks, wellies, and rain gear. I encased all equipment in dry bags, and was off by 9:20. First I walked the beach, and strolled past the grade school. Totem poles were in the front. There were a few houses and a Russian Orthodox church, which did not seem to be open. It was a birdy morning. One little tree held Dark-eyed Juncos, Golden-crowned Kinglets, and Orange-crowned Warblers. The big birds, Eagles, Ravens, and Crows, were higher over the water. Kootznahoo Road forked to the left, leading to Ramona's. When the rain began to pour, I ducked in for coffee and to change the film in my camera. BD time—(Before Digital). How much more complicated life was then! A woman named Nellie asked me if I had seen any bears yet. When I said "not yet" she began to tell me bear stories. It passed the time.

The only other road I found was Old Kootznahoo Road. It led to a small "trading post." There I purchased aspirin, a gourmet cream soda, and a Juneau newspaper. The rain stopped, so I hoofed it over to the dock and looked at gulls while I drank the soda. I sketched. It was peaceful. There is nothing like feeling alone in a wild place. The world seems enormous and wonderful.

Heading back to the B & B, I thought to myself that the place really should be called "Harold's." Sure enough, there was Harold, who was ready to chat again as I ate some grapes. He showed me his father's picture in a National Geographic. Then he turned on the TV to watch "Witness." I put on a hat to keep the rain from spotting my glasses, and escaped from the TV, back out into the wet.

I kicked along Kootznahoo in my wellies till I got to the dump. There were some cars there, but I didn't feel like lingering by the burning trash. I turned around and took a few steps . . . . and a brown bear loped easily across the road about 100 feet in front of me! I muttered an oath and *FROZE*. How lightly it moved, like a big fluff blowing across in the wind. But . . . 300 pounds of fluff—with claws! It disappeared into the fireweed to my right, so I had to walk past the spot where it had vanished. Why did I say I wanted to see a bear? It was all I could do not to dash to my room and lock the door. But as I neared the B & B, I relaxed a little and decided to sit on the seaplane dock. I saw a bear, all right. And not at the dump! Mission accomplished.

There were two Eagles fishing, and funny little White-winged Scoters swam about, low in the water, searching, I had read, for shell fish. They are able to stay under for quite a long time, then they fly, flapping vigorously, showing two white flashes. A small brown head appeared, followed by a wake. An otter! It shook its head, I heard it . . . *pfffff!* And then it dove. I am very fond of otters. Who isn't? I hit the jackpot that day for wildlife.

Once more Harold was in the B & B when I returned. The CB radio was on, announced that "Alberta's husband has been fishing on Elfin Cove and had experienced chest pains for two days." Prayers were requested, as well as donations of money so Alberta could reach him by ferry. Howard told me that was his sister speaking.

Since I planned to take the night ferry to Juneau, Harold told me, he would have to charge me $5 to drive me to the ferry dock (after hours fee). "Goin' to Juneau, eh?"

On the way, we stopped at the dump. He backed up, pulled in, up close and personal, and there were two of the hugest bears I've ever seen outside a glass case. The one that I had seen must have been a midget! I wondered where mama had been. While I gasped, Harold laughed like a crazy person. "Saw bears, eh?"

The ferry, called Le Conte, was buzzing with activity. Many teenagers came aboard just to buy a hamburger. I searched to find a seat. The side sections were filled with sleeping bags. After treating myself to a gourmet meal of a Snickers bar, a Diet Coke and a sleeping pill, I lay on the floor in the bow with my coat for a blanket and my sweatshirt for a pillow and slept soundly for four or five hours.

Le Conte's cafeteria opened at 7 the next morning. I got myself some scrambled eggs and toast and was half-way through eating when the captain announced "Humpback to port!" I grabbed my binoculars, abandoned my eggs and ran out onto the rain-soaked deck . . . and was rewarded! It was the best whale show ever.

The rain was relentless. The islands we passed were steel gray, some almost black; waters gray as well, so cold that to be in them for two minutes would kill you. The skies closed down over and in between the mountains and were still another shade of cold gray. Far ahead, one patch of open sky was blue and big enough to let the sun through. There, what a transformation! The mountains became the palest, purest blue/white, beckoning like a promise.

Le Conte reached Juneau by 11 a.m. The terminal was busy, full of loud talkers, and banging doors. I moved away from a leg tapper to two youngsters playing cards. It was still pouring. I mean *pouring.*

The connecting ferry to Haines, The Malaspina, boarded by 11:50. I wrote, *"Now this is a ferry! I'm up on top, little tables and chairs near the windows—I guess this is the best place. It's so darn big I don't want to take too much time exploring. I staked this place and will explore later. I did just happen to see . . . a gift shop! Oh, my."*

I went in the gift shop. I bought a paperback, a long-sleeved t-shirt, and some post cards that I never wrote. I still have that shirt, all these years later. It's nice and warm. I don't need warm shirts very often, living in South Florida. But it's been to other cold places!

Then the rain stopped. It was just a beautiful ride. There was a knowledgeable naturalist on board who chatted with me for a while about birds and other wildlife. She had worked on Admiralty Island for 10 years studying bears. On board, she pointed out Marbled Murrelets, Common Murre, Arctic Terns and Mew Gulls. Dall Porpoises made brief appearances. By the time the ferry arrived at Haines, the day was downright breathtaking. And there was John, waiting for the ferry to dock.

Haines was the first permanent army base in Alaska. Some 90 buildings were built in the early 1900's, including houses for officers and a hospital. At the end of World War II the base was closed. The buildings then became homes, shops, and cultural attractions. I found the row of old buildings charming and quite well kept.

John and I greeted each other as though we had seen each other only yesterday. We walked to his apartment. It was a senior citizen/low income facility called "Dusty Trails." He put my belongings in the one bedroom and said he would sleep in the living room. Then he took me out to Fort Seward Lodge along with a friend of his from Homer who was serving on a Coast Guard ship docked at Haines. Following dinner (oysters!), we took a walk around the old barracks. I met an artist friend of John's, and bought a carved whale at his shop. We walked, talked, and lo and behold, when we returned to "Dusty Trails," John offered me a glass of whiskey! I gladly accepted, and watched him in a new role. He drank a glass of water, then downed a shot of Jim Beam, while I sipped.

My Christmas card was hanging from a string in the living room, as usual. A rope served as towel holder in the bathroom. Another rope was strung from the towel holder to the shower curtain. This had clothespins clipped on it. A mop lay across the top of the medicine cabinet. A paper bag served as a wastebasket. John's "bed" in the living room was a piece of plywood supported by four plastic cartons. A piece of foam made the mattress. Everywhere, there were pieces of leather, cardboard boxes, and sure enough, his old stitching horse. For a tablecloth? A piece of newspaper. Some things hadn't changed. Except this time I had brought my own towel.

Plans for the next day included a trip across Canadian tundra and panning for gold.

The following morning, my alarm woke me at 6. I had hoped to wake before John, but was not successful. He was already making coffee and pouring orange juice. We went out for a walk down to the boat dock, where there were a few brave sail boats among the many fishing boats. John reckoned the weather to be questionable for our outing, so there was much judging of clouds and checking the weather by radio. We ate four-grain hot cereal with raisins and I had half and half on mine. John poured olive oil on his. I refrained from asking why.

A woman I'll call Sue had set up housekeeping next door to John. We paid a call. When she answered the door, she said, "Oh, dear, I haven't combed my hair yet." Her hair looked good to me. It was long and wavy; a lovely chestnut. But she let us in, gazing at me warily through big round glasses. John told me later I made a big mistake. I walked on her oriental rug with my boots on. Ooops. We discussed the proposed outing across the tundra. Sue was unavailable for that because she had a turkey in the oven. A turkey in the oven? On the morning of July 14? Again, I refrained from asking questions.

Sue was younger than I, and therefore much younger than John. She might have weighed a bit more than John. I guessed she had hopes of being important to him in some way. She seemed needy. John told me it took her 45 minutes to floss her teeth. I don't know how he knew that.

After John and I strolled around town for a bit, we stopped to see Sue again. She had by then combed her hair. We decided to postpone the Canadian tundra trip until the following day. Sue remarked that she would bring a turkey sandwich along for herself because she said she could not afford to buy lunch. "Oh, I'll buy lunch for us all," I said. I thought to myself, "OK, Marge, let's be tolerant of others," but wondered what percentage of folks in Alaska are far off the radar for normality. I found it intriguing in John but just plain weird in Sue.

That settled, John and I returned to his apartment for a lunch of wilderness food—still on John's menu though he now lived in town: hardtack, tea, and cheese. It suited me fine.

The afternoon turned out to be lovely. It seemed quite prefect to me. We walked down to Portage Cove State Recreation Area, where a man was mowing the grass by the tent area. Sitting and looking over the deep blue waters of the Cove, peace descended. By this time, the day was beautiful in the way only a clear day can be after days of steady rain. Dozens of hummingbirds were busy at the Fireweed, and not one bit shy. Sst, sst, sst, I heard, as well as their lightning fast wing strokes. Cones hung from the spruce trees, heavy from the rain and glistening in the sun. An Orange-Crowned warbler flew so close to me I had no use for binoculars. Then, for the first time in my life, I saw a Harlequin Duck, striking and gorgeous. What marvelous mysteries are the colors and patterns on birds. How lucky was I to see this masterpiece of design.

That evening at Dusty Trails, John fixed the strap on my hat, which I had been having trouble tightening enough to be useful. I said, "John, why didn't anyone else ever think of this?" He showed a twinkly grin and replied, "'Cause they're stupid." Well, that was rather harsh. So was his solution to problematic people: "Retroactive contraception."

As we ate some delicious peppery stew, John told me that senior residences in Alaska hold inspections twice a year to see if the rugged Alaskans are taking care of modern housing. I would have loved to know how John rated. OK, I guessed, since he was still living there. It made me wonder how bad a place would have to be for the resident to get evicted. Rent, John allowed, was 30 per cent of one's monthly income. Every resident in Alaska gets an oil allowance. No wonder there isn't a huge majority of conservationists. I wondered if the true ecologists turned down their allowance. One more question not asked. I should have been nosier.

Of course it was still light when our evening meal ended, so John chose to go out walking again. There were no fast food stores in town, and only one store had a name I knew: Radio Shack. There was one traffic light in the whole town. I loved it.

A cruise ship was in port. Oh, my goodness, John just loved to talk to these people. He was behaving like a Walmart greeter! He chatted up a family from Texas and mentioned his book, which was on sale at the bookstore (Babbling Book). The family ended up walking with us to the store and buying the book for John to autograph. I started talking books to Mrs. L. We discovered we both admired Clyde Edgerton, especially Walking Across Egypt. She said she had phoned Edgerton herself and expressed her love of the book. One thing led to another, and one young boy in the family invited us out to eat with them! John accepted with alacrity, to my surprise, and proceeded to eat another entire meal. This man amazed me. I had one oyster from Mr. L's plate and an Alaskan Amber beer (great combination). It seemed to be no hardship for them to treat us, as the lady of the family flashed a huge diamond.

I just couldn't understand John eating another entire meal. Hmmm . . . .

There was no sketching for me that day. Too busy. Sleep came easily. Waking the next morning was more difficult. I described it in my journal as *"an upward swim from sleep. John already up."*

It was the usual type of Alaska morning: overcast, gloomy, some rain. After eating oatmeal, we stopped in at the grocery store for supplies. John visited two "flight-seeing" offices to inquire about weather predictions. There were mixed reviews. A lengthy discussion ended with the decision to go to Canada and visit a gold mine.

Sue was slow to ready herself, but we got underway around 11. What a fine day it turned out to be! We drove north toward Haines Junction with the gray Chilcat River to the west. I was told that Chilcat means "catch fish." John's vehicle was an '82 Ford wagon. It was an awesome drive—snowcapped mountains all around. Cottonwoods were dropping white fluff. The spruces were heavy with cones.

At Mile 33 we stopped at a well-known hamburger joint. Barn swallows were driving all over the place. One posed prettily on a set of antlers over the door. Pine siskins hopped about, and hummingbirds zoomed to and from the feeders outside the windows. John spoke to other people in the restaurant, attempting to build interest in his book.

We passed through to Canada easily. There certainly were no lines of traffic, and passports were not required. Shortly we entered the Yukon! Tatshenshini-Alsek Wilderness Provincial Park! I was excited about this, especially since I hadn't expected this additional treat. We stopped above the tree line hill to take a picture, and met up with two bikers. One fellow was from New Zealand; the other from Holland. Their story must have been an interesting one, as I am sure they thought John's and mine must be, but we didn't take time to chat . . . . just took each others' pictures. My mind was spinning with the weirdness of the moment. There I was, at the "top of the world," and I knew that at the same time, my son and his wife were in New Zealand.

A quote from St. Augustine came to find: "The world is a book and those who do not travel read only one page."

Back in the car, a young bear, "rocking-chair galloped," as John said, before us. A sign announced that we were on the Historic Dalton Trail that gold miners used. A bit farther on, John announced that we had gone about as high as we could go, so we turned around and re-entered the U.S.

The next stop was Porcupine Gold Mine via a gravel road. In five hours we might have seen three other cars. Yet when we arrived at the mine, it was like old home week. I certainly never knew how John was acquainted with Irma, the wife of the mine owner, but it seemed like they were old friends. "Sure, have a look around," she said. "Go watch the clean-up!"

This was the clean-up of the day's diggings. Water and gravel ran through a series of bending chutes, like a waterfall. I was told the gold sinks to the bottom, while the gravel keeps on going with the water. And it was mighty cold water, too, I noted in passing. A young guy who looked a lot like Chuck Norris was scooping the gold flakes and chunks from the bottom of the run. He let us feel the weight of the gold. The noise of the Porcupine River roaring past at great speed made it necessary for us to shout.

Sue retired to the porch with Irma. She did not want to try to pan for gold as John suggested. I looked at her hands. She had huge rings on most fingers. Perhaps they would have interfered. John led me to the panning table. He panned like an artist, moving the pan back and forth gracefully, spilling out the gravel and silt and allowing the gold dust to sink to the bottom of the pan. I found it tricky in the extreme to spill off the silt while allowing the gold dust to remain. It was pre-digital days. I dug out an empty film canister (weren't they the most useful things?) and John spilled the gold dust he had found into it. He said it might be worth 10 cents. Still, I kept it, and have it still.

Irma offered us coffee, which we gladly accepted. Sue whispered to me, "I wish John didn't have to have so many women!" I had no reply to that. I did wonder what people thought was going on between John and me. Or between John and Sue, for that matter. We said good-by to Irma and climbed into the car. The afternoon sun slanted through the trees and lit up the rock faces and snow fields. We twisted around a small lake, where a Red-Breasted Merganser and five ducklings swam about. The drive back never stopped being lovely.

John prepared halibut and a salad for dinner on our return, followed by some Jim Beam. Talk about a perfect day.

But wait, it wasn't over yet. We took a short walk to "see Bill." There was a small ship in harbor, but no one was about, and all the shops were closed. We returned to Dusty Trails. John put on some Russian music, of which he was fond, and fell asleep. I washed my hair.

My suggestion of a train trip to Skagway was scheduled for the following day. There, as my treat, we planned to take the "scenic railway of the world" along the Yukon Route to White Pass. First, we took a "water taxi" that left from Haines. As John and I stood on the upper deck, a young fellow from Australia and a girl from Seattle began chatting us up. John abruptly left. Here was another contradiction in his social ability. No explanation was offered. Perhaps he needed a restroom.

Skagway turned out to be extremely touristy, with a capital T. Three cruise ships were docked there. Colorful sweat suits abounded. There were horse-drawn carriages and many shops. I noted a sign in a jewelry store: "Lost wives found here." There was a book in one window named Catch and Release: A Guide to Alaska Men.

We looked in at a museum. John used the rest room and then we watched a movie about the 1898 gold rush, narrated by Hal Holbrook. It was informative and entertaining. The sheer number of people who attempted the trek for gold was amazing. The conditions were severe beyond imagination.

We ate at some kind of "sourdough" restaurant. At 11:40, we were the only ones in the place. Ten minutes later it was full. Cruise ship schedules, I guessed. The food was hearty and appealing. While we were eating, I decided to try to interview John. I was a great fan of Inside the Actors Studio at the time, especially James Lipton's use of the interview questions of Bernard Pivot (actually based on ideas of Marcel Proust). I used an abbreviated version.

What is your favorite sound?	*Wind in the spruce*
What is your least favorite sound?	*Loud conversation*
What is your favorite word?	*Peace*
What is your least favorite word?	*War*
What is your favorite curse word?	*John said he curses, but he wouldn't say a curse word to me.*
What makes you "high?"	*When someone I regard highly tells me that they regard me highly, too*
If heaven exists, what would you like to hear God say when you arrive at the Pearly Gates?	*Well done, good and faithful servant.*

He didn't ask me what my answers would be.

OK. It was time to board the train. There was a "slight" change. One of the trains was not operating. A kind lady told us we could ride a bus up the Chilcoot Pass to White Pass and then take a train back down White Pass to Skagway. I was all ready to be upset, but this turned out to be a good deal. We actually got views of the pass from two sides, plus a gift certificate for $20 at the gift shop. Off we went.

The White Pass and Yukon Route has been declared an International Historic Civil Engineering Landmark for good reasons. The rides absolutely defied description, especially when I tried to imagine conquering this route on foot or horseback in search of gold. The route climbs 2,865 from Skagway in just 20 miles. One can see trails leading off from the road and the railroad tracks; hardy (foolhardy?) people still can hike them.

In the official brochure I found some astounding facts: "Before the railroad was built, prospectors trekked up with some disastrous results. Three thousand pack animals met their end in Dead Horse Gulch in 1898. Those gold-seekers who reached the U.S./Canadian border were allowed across only if they had a ton of supplies (literally)—enough to survive in the North for a year. Workers hung suspended by ropes from vertical cliffs, blasting and hacking their way through granite walls. Heavy snows and temperatures as low as 60 below hampered the work."

Reading the facts was one thing—experiencing the journey, albeit in a comfortable seat, was quite another. Once again, adjectives seemed trivial. Amazing and astounding are over-used. The ride was spectacular. Waterfalls, bridges over gulches designed to expand in case of earthquakes, tunnels, at last the summit. John fell asleep.

Another water taxi ride took us back to Haines, where, according to my journal, we had *"Jimmy Boy Beam, rye tack, and cheese."* I was ready to mellow out, but John announced that he "took a notion" to visit Bill, whom John described as a "pretty skookum kind of guy." That meant he was strong and attractive. We walked down to Bill's place, which was an Alaskan Native art shop. Bill, indeed, was strong and attractive. At one point he said to me with a sly look, "How are you and Sue getting along?" I grinned back and replied, "Oh, we're like sisters." Bill opined, "I think you and Sue are opposite personalities." Quickly, I replied, "Thank you!"

I asked Bill some of the Lipton questions:

His favorite word:	pulchritude
His least favorite word:	curses
His favorite sound:	Too many—depends on the time of day
His least favorite sound:	Didn't have any. (Whew, I could tell he didn't live in a big city!)
What he wanted to hear when he entered Heaven:	"I know her already. Everything will be fine."

Bill did not ask for my answers.

I was tired and wanted to leave. Eventually, we did.

I wrote in my journal, *"J seems out of sorts. Much grunting and farting. Withdraws from time to time. Likes to draw attention to himself."* I was stupid. The man was not well.

The next morning I "slept in" until 6:30. John "repaired" my rain parka with contact cement. I noted that my coat "smelled like a toxic dump." We walked to the grocery store where John got a 55 cent refund on his $5.50 bill because it was "senior" day. Alaska treats its seniors well! We passed a building that said "Alaska Nature Tours," and I inquired about their programs and remarked that I'd enjoy meeting a local birder. John opened the door that said "Closed" and walked right in. A voice said, "That sounds like John Ireland." And so I met Daniel. His schedule did not leave him free for guiding me. However, he did give me some pointers. Then we were on our way.

What next? A hike up Mount Ripinsky. Not a good choice. First of all, we walked a good two miles through road work, firewood cutting and hauling, to reach the trail head. The work was being done because (shudder) a 54-house development was being built. We sat amongst the road machinery to eat rye tack and cheese. No water. Big mistake. This definitely was not the wilderness, where we could find salmonberries for juice.

When we finally got on the trail, John cut me an alder walking stick, because I fell. It was a difficult trail for me . . . . many roots, steep, Devil's Club (ouch). It was 1.5 miles to the first overlook and we never made it. It was very hot. John stated that he was "tired of that trail." When he suggested that we turn back, I readily agreed. Since John could not hear the birdsong, he never stopped to look, so I didn't, either. I needed to concentrate on my feet, anyway. I staggered back I don't know how many miles to Dusty Trails, took two aspirin and drank a cup of tea.

John decided to go out and buy raisins and "see Bill." He looked at me and guessed that I "wouldn't want to walk any more tonight." He was so right. I nodded. John downed one glass of water and a shot of Jim Beam and was out the door.

While John was out, I picked up a copy of the Chilkat Valley News, a weekly newspaper in Haines, and read the following:

PLANNERS FLESH OUT ZONING:

Planning and zoning needn't be boring. A draft revision of the City's land use ordinance lists, among other allowable uses, "nudist colony." It's right in there with home occupation, bed and breakfast, kennel, and correctional facility.

The requirement for "nudist colony:" Must be near and in view of council person's house. The draft document doesn't address whether departure from code would require a variance or a deviance.

City administrator Tom Healy confirmed that the City's consultants inserted that joke to see if the draft really was getting read by policy makers.

Public hearings on the comprehensive plan are expected by September.

The following day brought relentless rain. Despite the foul weather, after a morning inside, we ventured out. While we walked toward Portage Cove Park, John admitted that yesterday he had "overextended himself." I asked him twice if he wanted to turn back. The reply was negative. Then he informed me that we were *walking* to Dalton City . . . six miles away. I suppose at that time I didn't know enough (again) to ask the right questions.

Dalton City was a movie set for White Fang. After the movie was made, the set remained in place and became a sort of tourist destination. Ptarmigan Press, the outfit that had printed John's book, occupied one of the buildings. Another popular place was the Klondike Bar, where we enjoyed Alaska Amber, chili, and chips. John was truly doing his best to show me around during my last two days in Alaska. My wellies had been of great use. But I must say, those last few days in Alaska had no comparison to Murder Lake, and I felt great sympathy for John, that he had to give up his wilderness existence and retreat to "town" life because of his age and health.

The next day we hit the grocery store. I had determined early on to buy John a new dishwashing scrubber brush. His was absolutely worn to the nubs. It had bristles about ¼ of an inch long and was caked with black goo down to the pink handle. I bought it on the sly while he scrutinized 19-cents-a-pound rotting bananas. Alaska is a long distance from banana trees. When we returned to his apartment, I asked him if he was attached to his dish scrubber. "Yes!" he replied, "I scrub dishes with that!" "Well," I responded, "I bought you a new one. I thought you could use one." His answer? "Oh, that was nice of you. I guess this one is not too sanitary. I'll keep it, retire it, but might be good for something like cleaning boots." Exactly!

The filthy weather (as my British cousins call it) continued. We lunched at the Chilkat Restaurant and Bakery. My treat, but John chose the restaurant. Good choice. Bikers were eating there. I heard heavy accents: "I might gist git one of them t-shir-uts. Reckin I cn cram one more thang in that bag." Two ladies shared jokes with

John. I don't remember any of them, but they all had a good time. So did I.

The afternoon was spent at Sheldon Museum. It was very pleasant, and I learned that eagles mate for life. The rain continued.

Alas, the next morning it continued to rain. Sue, whom we had not seen for days, stopped by. She was having poor luck in the romantic department. A dinner date had been cancelled so that the fellow could go subsistence fishing. Sue invited us to her place for a game of Scrabble if we "promised to take our shoes off before we trod on her oriental carpet." We agreed.

After the game of Scrabble, which Sue won, the day morphed into perfection! What a gift! John and I decided to visit Chilcoot Lake. Sue did not want to go, because she was "tired."

Journal:

We saw eagle, kingfisher, red-breasted and Common Merganser, with a dozen ducklings. How beautiful they are, crests blowing in the breeze, russet necks, fluidly flipping head first, body following like an "s" to get fish. The Chilcoot River, as we neared the lake, became rushing and white, passing the rocks downstream.

Fishermen, standing in the erect serenity that says "I'll wait." Then the lake, still a glacial mirror, waterfalls tumbling down looking like nothing more than white threads down the distant peaks. A walk through the park, quiet and thick, with layers of spruce and hemlock needles.

John talked to the guys fishing. One said, "Why aren't you fishing?" John replied, "Well, I don't need any fish." Dead silence followed.

We drove around the lake to see what at first appeared to be a huge patch of seaweed. It turned out to be hundreds of surf and white-winged scoters, and a harbor seal, balanced on a rock, yawning. It was a wonder-full world, one I never would have seen but for a chance meeting on a bus: John.

Upon our return to Haines, I invited John and Sue to dinner, my treat. I had been salivating for steamed oysters and Alaska Amber since tasting those the other night. Sue was not too tired to join us.

As we ate, I asked Sue the Lipton questions:

Her favorite sound:	a wine cork popping
Her least favorite sound:	bacon frying
Her favorite word:	love
Her least favorite word:	betrayal
What made her feel "high:"	playing with her cats
What she wanted to hear when entering Heaven:	You're forgiven.

Sue did not ask for my responses.

Surprisingly, I did make note that I asked John this question: How in the world did a guide/hunter get a moose head out of the woods? He replied that one removes the antlers and skins the head. He added, "Europeans want the whole skull and even some teeth." A partial answer, and that's all I got.

We walked around Haines after dinner. A man the locals called "Crow Man" was roaming around town, mumbling. He feeds the crows and tells everyone to have a wonderful day.

John told me he had made a plan to go to Murder Lake with two other women in August! What a surprise. Lucky them, I thought. And good for John that he would be able to visit that special place. I admit I was envious, and still trying to compute his comments that he "didn't seek out female company." Later, through our correspondence, I learned I needn't have felt any remorse about not "going back."

The following morning, we awoke at 6. I packed, had coffee, orange juice, and oatmeal, and decided to walk around town so that I could say my good-byes. John remarked that he didn't feel that well. We chatted with a woman whom John described as "a nice gal, but kind of a heathen." I wondered what he would think of me if I had been more honest. For years, I had characterized John as a man of contradictions, but had to admit that he would think the same of me. We shared the one undeniable link with the natural world. It was my luck that I had met this man who could show me a side of that world I never would have known otherwise, and for that, he earned my lasting gratitude.

Then, through conversations with others in town, we learned that my plans for departing Haines had been complicated by politics! Canadians were fighting for a fair portion of the Pacific Salmon catch that they shared with U.S. fleets. A wall of fishing boats had surrounded "my" ferry in Prince Rupert and would not let it proceed to Haines, where I was supposed to board it for Juneau. I had to make a hurried decision. Should I fly to Juneau, or take a ferry that was presently docked in Haines and would leave at 10:15 p.m. I opted for the late departing ferry.

Thus we had more time together. John opined, "Seems like more girls are going to college these days. I think they don't mind being preached to." I replied, "John it's because men think they already know everything!" Then we had a long debate about "teaching" versus "preaching." It was one of our most honest conversations.

Then to add to the complications, on the way to the ferry that night, the road was partially blocked by a rock slide! But, I made it. Both of us felt awkward. I gave John a big hug and tried my best to thank him. The ferry left at midnight. In the distance, John looked so little, as we all do against the huge landscape that is Alaska. And I knew he was ill and weakening.

The ferry arrived in Juneau at 4:30 a.m. A van arrived to take me to my motel, where I fell into bed fully clothed and fell asleep. No time to be emotional. That would come later. I had scheduled an all-day Tracy Arm excursion for that same morning, and had to be up at 7.

Journal:

Am presently sitting in a restaurant sipping a glass of Merlot and waiting for my body to stop weaving from the all-day excursion, and further waiting for my nose to stop being cold. These are the words I composed at sea: It was a forbidding day. Clouds were draped low and wound around the mountains, other clouds lay thick, just above the choppy gray waters. Rain fell relentlessly, through every mile the boat progressed. The rain didn't slant, or blow, or pour: it fell. Every now and then the sky and horizon was a little less gray, but the sun was not seen today. Clouds lay in horizontal layers, and it was cold. (Just now I see a woman outdoors in a sleeveless jersey. Is she from Iceland?) It is July! All of this lent an air of otherworldliness to this glacier excursion. Through the mist we saw a humpback. Patiently standing in the cold rain paid off: spume, breach, spume, breach, and then, the tail waved, huge and black.

It was a long ride out, away from Juneau, but I had the best seat mate: a silent watcher, like me. No small talk."

I just sat back and drank in the surroundings and the mood—which remained harsh and unforgiving, to humans, if not harbor seals, who sat, seemingly contentedly, on small icebergs, objecting only to the proximity of the noise of the boat. They are creatures of undeniable charm and stamina. We passed steep walls of nearly vertical rock. Waterfalls spewed great quantities of water from them, but seen from such a distance, and originating from such a height, the appeared as narrow threads, like veins of precious metal. Birds were everywhere: pigeon guillemot, scoters, murrelets, gulls, loons, and terns. The glaciers: Is there a way to describe the color? The blue? The variations? Only glacial. If you've not seen it, you don't know.

My departure from Alaska was abrupt, but on the plane I had plenty of time to reflect and write:

Journal—Seattle: noon—But 11 my internal time.

John is probably walking about in Haines; somebody else is out on the Inside Passage, looking at glaciers; and many are fishing in Chilcoot Lake. Now that I'm in the lower 48, I see more minority groups, baggie trousers, sunglasses, more folks wearing fewer clothes. I feel somewhat vulnerable without my boots and three shirts. Coat packed last minute at Juneau airport. More noise. More rushing.

While I stayed with John, I looked at his few pictures again— John Denver and some of his hunt pictures. John's beard was a lot darker then, and he was skinny and rugged. What a strong, able person he was. He is now given to taking deep breaths and puffing after walking up a steep hill and much coughing. He eats Fisherman's Friends cough drops like candy. Much clearing of throat and flatulence. I suspect he doesn't hear the latter. Bending over is difficult, and a few pulls on his found rowing machine is all he accomplishes before another puff. He still outwalks me easily. He refuses to bow to his diminishing capacities, physically or mentally. That may be why he is so dogmatic in his conversation. He's insisting he still knows what he once knew. But he is forgetful. His hearing is spotty. He hears the clip-clop of one horse from inside his apartment; hears very little birdsong, can still hear a Cessna and identify its type; while listening to music he marvels at its beauty when in fact the tape is filled with static. Conversation is the most annoying and difficult for him. I asked him if he thought shooting had worsened his hearing. "Yes" was the firm answer. I figure one of Sue's main attractions seems to be her voice. Mine doesn't seem to be in the range he hears anymore, especially when I raise my voice to make it audible. So conversations between us are strained. Questions and answers are easiest, when three or four try a conversation, it's impossible. John doesn't hear another's sentence, and speaks at the same time. Since he tends to repeat himself, the perception is that he constantly interrupts others. After a while, I'd just give up.

The habits of the wilderness (camp dishes, newspapers for tablecloths, saving everything like glass jars) which seemed colorful at Murder Lake, just seemed sad in Haines. A broom secured by the front door was good in the Talkeetnas but silly in town. Same with the mop hanging over the shower. 1996 newspapers could easily be replaced by at least 1997 editions, since there's a 3-foot pile of newspapers in the corner of his living room. He's got huge closets with not much in them, because everything is hanging from walls. There was a shovel on top of the kitchen cabinets. Habits of a lifetime don't change easily.

When people meet John, I can see my own initial reaction to his story in them. And it's still a story to hear. It's just so sad to see John translated into town life and becoming a cruise passenger groupie. He's so authentic in the woods—knows plants, tracks, ways of rivers and tides—he's a genius. Because he is so wise in the ways of natural life, he assumes he's that way—or has the authoritative air about him—of all other matters. What astounds me is that he seems indifferent to the wonder surrounding him. A certain amount of that is inevitable, I suppose. But he told me his purpose of life is the glorification of God. Well, if you're a religious person, I would expect you to take joy at most times in mountains, flowers, trees, rivers, animals—that your deity has created. John doesn't seem to any more. Mount Ripinsky was "boring." I questioned him about his repeated statements, in letters, that he saw no purpose in life. He seemed surprised that he had said that and had no real answer. He said humanity is disgusting and there's no hope. But he has friends and is very sociable. I questioned him about that, too. Well, he admitted, some people are good. I wondered if I was one. He's worried about one friend who kept "removing" herself from conversation to go play solitaire on a computer. He can't stand "meaningless chatter" but is pretty good at it himself.

John had spent his life becoming—building the persona—of the backwoods huntsman and hermit. One time he berated someone for writing a biography. "It's a vain act." Now that his role has changed, he goes around telling his life and pushing sales of his book. Where has the strong, independent loner gone? Why does he so much want to teach others about the outdoors, and so much resents the efforts of others to teach by calling it "preaching?" The inconsistencies in his personality cannot completely be attributed to age.

So heroes diminish upon close inspection . . . become humans like oneself, and so I see that I am not unique in receiving invitations to visit the wilderness, so I diminish in importance as well.

It remains that the experiences John has made possible for me are beyond anything I'd possibly dreamed of. For that I am forever grateful. Gratitude is a particular kind of love.

Once again, I re-entered my life in Fort Lauderdale. Shortly afterwards, our correspondence continued.

After thanking him, of course, for his hospitality, and the opportunity to see yet another location in Alaska, I mentioned that it was a real mental chore, getting used to 90-degree heat. It was. He replied: *"gratified that you apparently had an enjoyable trip/visit. And it was good for me to have a visitor, especially one like you, among the very few who would really care about me.*

Here's what John had to say about his return to Murder Lake: *"At Murder Lake we saw nothing except a couple of Beaver. We were there for a week, and it rained four days of it. Lake level and creeks were very high; too high to cross creeks with hip boots. It's like the country is under a curse, between the Indian ownership and the greedy town dudes. Lake Dame Nature is showing disapproval; She never let me down (until this time). Never when I needed Her, did she fail me. It is unlikely I'll return to Murder Lake; the Fishing seems ruined, and I doubt it'd rebuild, even with most strict protective measures, and those observed, if ever, but notably within years remaining in which I'd be able to fish. So goes another of few joys in life remaining to me, overcome by the greed for money and noticeability on the part(s) of some who are not on the side of the wilderness environment. It's sickening."*

I commiserated with him about "going back" to places much loved. My own example was St. Lucia, which I had visited when I was married. It was so stunningly beautiful that I have since been afraid to go back. It couldn't have been as gorgeous and unspoiled as it was when I was there. I remembered looking at those twin volcanic peaks, eating fresh lobster, and swimming to visit a couple in their yacht after primo snorkeling. I'm fairly confident that had little relevance to John, but I tried.

My only news that October was that I had purchased a new car (still have it!) and my son and daughter-in-law were due back from their trip around the world. Huge stuff for me, but of little interest to John.

Then came news of John having chest pains. The ladies in his life took care of him and urged him to see a doctor, against his usual approaches to illness. He had many tests, and was prescribed medications, to which he responded well, and then seemed to dismiss any possibility of serious illness.

I went to North Carolina with a friend and enjoyed the autumn colors; had a look at "my land," a referral I disliked using since becoming familiar with John's opinion that land ownership was faulty and should be described as "prior use." The dream of a cabin was fading fast, but I didn't pay much in annual taxes for the land, so I kept it.

Next thing I knew, John was entering into a real new-age stage of development. He was seeing an acupuncturist for the chest pains. He declared that the chest pains had been caused by a lack of joy of living coupled with anger which caused "a Chi stoppage." I had no idea what that meant. In the long term, nothing much worked to ease him of his growing number of symptoms. He spent Thanksgiving alone, refusing all offers of going out for a meal or having one of his neighbor ladies bring him food.

By Christmas 1997, he was somewhat better physically, but emotionally, he complained a lot in his letters: noisy neighbors, lack of appetite, neediness of his neighbor Sue, etc. He did thank me for the weather radio I sent him via L.L.Bean, and reiterated that he did not give gifts. It brought to my mind all the unique gifts he had given me in the form of allowing me to visit Alaska as few others have the opportunity to do. He was happy to accept a pot of turkey soup from the lady at Porcupine Mine; and a TV from another female friend. It was good he had ladies to look after him.

My days that December were contented. Of all the good luck! My son and his wife were back from their round the world trip, and he accepted a job in South Florida! They bought a house five minutes away from me.

Then . . . . months of silence from Alaska.

I found Sue's address in my scrapbook, and wrote to her. She answered that John was very ill, and had moved back to Homer. She said that was all she knew, for he had abruptly terminated their friendship.

In March, I tried writing to John's friends in Homer. They were the first of his friends he introduced to me, the ones who ran the antique shop in Homer where John sold some of his leather work. I had that address from a receipt they had given me when I bought one of his leather boxes. The letter was returned to me. It was marked "forward expired." So I surmised that the antique shop was closed. Alas, this was in the days before email was common, and I knew that the only place John had ever had a telephone was at Dogfish Bay.

To my surprise, I received a long letter at the end of the month from the very people I had tried to contact in Homer. It read,

"John Ireland has asked me to write you and tell you about what has been happening with him the last few months. Your letter of February 2 was forwarded to Homer last week and you expressed concern for his welfare. As you suspected, he has been ill. Late in January the clinic in Haines sent him to the hospital in Juneau

for what they thought was anemia which was failing to respond to treatment. In Juneau he was diagnosed with bacterial endocarditis, an infection of the heart lining. This condition damages heart valves, and it did exactly that to at least one of John's.

He was sent from Juneau in early February to Anchorage for assessment for valve surgery. By mid Feb. his condition had deteriorated and he was no longer a good candidate for surgery. This was when I began to connect seriously with what was going on. I visited him in Anchorage at the end of February and found him in what I felt was very fragile condition. He seemed depressed, was not speaking, had lost a great deal of weight, couldn't (or wouldn't) eat. His doctors there felt that he had decided to die, and his friends in Anchorage talked to John's Homer physician who said, 'By all means, bring John to Homer.' As you know, John has a wide circle of friends here, and has especially strong connections among the staff at the hospital as a result of his volunteer efforts there.

I am very happy to be able to report that John's condition has improved greatly in the three weeks he has been here. He is able to eat a few bites, is able to walk into the hall by his room, and is able to talk sparingly, but normally. He never lost his ability to make decisions for his care, but he has so little strength and energy I am attending to his business affairs for him. His normal dislike for the telephone has increased and he is not talking to people by phone, but I will be happy to talk to you if you have any questions. (She gave me an address where I could write to John and said she and her husband visited him every day.)

In mid-April Jim and I plan to go to Haines and move his things back to Homer. When he is ready to move out of the hospital, we do not know if he will come to be with us or go to a care facility of some sort. At this time it looks as if it will be a long time before he again able to live alone.

I am sorry to have to give you this unpleasant news about our mutual friend, but at this time things are greatly improved. We still have the risk of the damaged valve giving way entirely, but unless he can regain his appetite and eat enough to gain some weight and strength, he is not a good candidate for even the high risk cardiac surgery available in Seattle. I will be sure to let you know if there is any dramatic change in John's condition."

Toward the end of June, I received a truly sad letter from John. It was obvious to me that the envelope had been printed by someone else, and inside was a weak scrawl that was difficult to make out. The doctors diagnosed a stroke. He said he had lost the ability to read and walk. He had also lost many memories. He had been with his friends in Homer for four months. *"They have apparently more faith in my complete recovery than I do,"* he managed to put on paper.

My mind was full of memories of hiking for hours with John through rough terrain; of steadily paddling with him in the canoe at Murder Lake; the hours of digging under that waterfall at Dogfish Bay; of his fierce independence. I wept and felt helpless.

His friends were wonderful, taking him in, seeing to his therapy and bills. *("I could not cope (sic) with any of that.")* Because he had lost many memories and could no longer read, an occupational therapist was helping him with that, and he believed typing on his old machine would help. It did. The next few letters were typewritten. There were many mistakes, but it was clear he was making progress. He appreciated my short notes because he grew tired with the effort of reading. His old irascibility came through a bit: *It seems like those people whose company I had troubled to cultivate, to any degree, have been kind . . . except Sue; she became boldly apparent in true colors, during time I was ill, still at Haines. I snapped it off, with her."* I could only wonder what on earth had happened. It was not worth bothering him about at this point in his recovery. His short one-page, double spaced letters, ended with *"Weariness overcomes, J."* But he continued to write! Ours was a friendship that defied most definitions.

By August John had moved into an assisted living residence in Homer. His typing and reading were improving, and he planned to undergo cataract surgery. Once again he had his leatherwork tools with him, and was thinking about teaching leatherwork to a *"fine-looking physical therapist who worked with me while in hospital."* He told me that she was 39 years old, single, and that she had a cat that *"took to me extraordinarily."* The man was surely consistent in his inconsistencies!

He also asked me to contact my family in England to find out about some "shoe thread" that he needed for his leatherwork. It seems he couldn't find a supplier. One of my cousin's husbands owned a mill, so I wrote to her—mostly in desperation—to see if I could possibly be of help in any way, from long-distance.

I received one letter in which he declared he *was "on the verge of entertaining some unpleasant thoughts about the English—I suspect they're working a sneak tactic to monopolize leather hand stitching by cutting off America from an essential supply. Troublemakers I don't need."*

Finally in September, he let me know that he had heard from my cousin about a supplier. And in time he did receive a supply of the thread. Whew! Thank goodness. I hadn't added to his dissatisfaction with life, which was obvious from the cranky nature of his letters. He complained about food, about expectations of others, even about the weather. *"Not feeling good today. Hell; been so long since I felt good can't even remember."* The one bright spot in his days seemed to be that good-looking leatherwork student of his! Good for him, I thought. But so unexpected from a loner who had lived in the wilderness for so long.

In March he reported with some pride that he had made himself some sourdough waffles!

His improvement was unbelievable to me, after seeing that first scrawled letter when he was so sick. Stroke—cancer—loss of vision—none of them had conquered him totally. Yes, he was cranky, but he tended to be that way when he was well. At least intolerant and impatient. And so he was with himself. It must have been terribly difficult to live having to depend on friends, however well-meaning they were.

Meanwhile, I was beginning to feel my age, as retirement neared. Two friends died unexpectedly, my mother's health continued to deteriorate, and I pretty much knew that I'd never see John again. His letters did not cheer me up at all.

Then, of all things, he wrote to tell me that he had returned to Murder Lake with his young student friend! The dentist flew them in. She wanted to learn how to fly cast.

"We spent two nights in the old cabin. The fishing was disappointing. There were some, but not many. I'd tied 3 flies— pleased to discover I could still do that—and caught fish with them. We kept no fish, there were so few. I could scarcely navigate the conditions. Now I am so weak, and get sooo tired. I am not content with what remains in life for me. Perhaps I should be grateful that I'm better off than some others."

What must have been his thoughts? How difficult it is to go back. But he was right. How lucky he was to be at Murder Lake again! So many memories came back to me. How lucky was I that I had been there. That trout that sparkled and the caribou's antlers glowed in the sun. The feeling of being small against the silent mountains.

John ailed. I planned a trip to Trinidad, to see colorful, fabulous birds at Asa Wright. I went by myself and joined up with three other women for hikes with a guide. It was exciting and as different from Alaska as possible. I felt helpless to assist John in any way, and felt I'd better travel as long as I was able, just as John had lived in the wilderness as long as he was able. He said each day when he woke, it was something of a surprise, and not necessarily a pleasant one. *"Way it seems life doesn't hold much anymore—but, looking around, I suppose I should be thankful for more blessings than some others around. But I think that's not the way life is supposed to be. In the wild, a disabled creature doesn't survive."* Nevertheless, he seemed to be surrounded by friends old and new who attempted to keep him interested in life. They took him to visit other friends in Seldovia and Haines. Alaskans seem to me to revere older people more than elsewhere. Well, especially in South Florida, where they're mostly laughed at by the general population.

It was 1999. I was 59 years old and purchased my first word processor. Hurricane Irene hit Fort Lauderdale. Teachers were not dismissed from school in time to tend to their window shutters. Two power poles went down on my street. My house was not damaged, but the yard required major cleaning up.

John's letters became more and more disheartening: *"I feel like the mule walking around bumping into things; people watching believed the mule was blind, but the owner said 'that mule's not blind, he just don't give a dam.'"*

Then, it was 2000. John was marking time until he "wouldn't be around;" Yet in other letters he still would be planning to purchase flax thread and leather so that he could teach his students his particular leatherworking skills. One supplier actually did reply to John, said they had the thread, but they sold it only in $600 lots. John wrote, "That is ca. 130-years' supply for one who uses it at the rate I do." He thought about writing a grant application to found a school to teach the "ancient method."

I was looking forward to retirement, which, I must say, I had carefully planned to occur when I was 62, the same year I would complete 30 years of service to Broward County Schools, and my mortgage would be paid. My career as a teacher was ending, but my civic activism was revving up. My neighbors and I were converting a weedy, undeveloped lot into a park. This involved writing grants, changing zoning, and landscaping. Years later riding past that park still stirs my feelings of pride in the accomplishment.

John wrote me to thank me for a "jumbo pen" I had sent him. *"Jumbo pen from you rec., thank you. When I was in hospital I really needed one like that; I had practically lost ability to handwrite. I remember thinking at the time, if I only had a thicker pen."*

In April, I wrote from my Head Start classroom.

Dear John,

I am writing this on my computer at school. There are seventeen four—and five-year old students napping on mats in my classroom. Everything seems peaceful.

Glad you like the pen. Here's a story. My mother has macular degeneration and already has had two cataract operations. She is 89, and has had a great deal of trouble seeing, especially when she writes, since the arthritis in her hands is advanced and she can't press very hard. She went in for a check-up at the ophthalmologist's office and went to the desk to sign in. She became upset when she couldn't manage the task, rang the bell, and told the receptionist she just couldn't do it. The receptionist (probably in her twenties) said, "Oh, I forgot! That pen doesn't work!"

Easter comes early this year. Teachers here are longing for spring break. I suppose after Easter the rest of the year will go by in a flash. One of my friends retired last week, and I must say I am somewhat envious. Families are less and less stable, as is society, and children are therefore more and more difficult to handle. Then the government steps in and hands down more and more requirements for teachers to fulfill in order to make up for the gaps in parental training. Can you believe I received a unit on the CENSUS that I am supposed to teach to four-year-olds?

His letters ranged from complaints about physical limitations to planned arrangements for the future. Mine ranged from thoughts of ending my teaching career to future plans for civic activism. And my mother's thoughts? I don't know. She was always cheerful, but not introspective. John was always introspective, but hardly ever cheerful. Me? I was not old enough to reach the state of introspection that age brings to a person, I guess.

Then, in April, the" cruelest month", John wrote

"I have become convinced I'm not going to get better. I feel so lousy all the time—it's anemia—life at this level is unsatisfactory. I'm going to quit trying. Get a couple things completed, I'm ready to throw in the towel."

My neighbors and I planted 250 trees in our new park. John opined *"such work as you and neighbors did, about the park . . . I used to be scornful towards people who could lie down and sleep beside a job that needed doing; now I have become one of them, though the spirit is willing, the flesh is weak. I do very little any more.*

I had a party for my mother's 90th birthday. One of my friends asked her if she had any advice. She replied *"You have to have a good sense of humor and a good appetite."*

Alas, John apparently had neither. He said his pain pills caused loss of appetite; his friends, although they sought his company, seemed to sit quietly and wait for 'words of wisdom.' He added, *"I have a hard time getting up interest in much of anything anymore. But it's not a bad life; at least free from the Great Joke of vital years: Sex."* That marks the first time he even mentioned that aspect of life. I was absolutely astonished, and glad that he said it in a letter, for if we had been sitting in the same room, I don't know what I would have replied. Had he ever thought of me in a sexual way? Not to my knowledge. I passed on the opportunity to respond in my next letter. He continued to write lovingly about his leather-work student. Her husband was out of town frequently, so she spent a lot of time with John. Perhaps that's why the subject of sex arose. Who knows?

In May, 2001, John reported feeling "terrible." *"I hope to have left a good impression on Earth."*

I replied quickly, *"You should know that many people, including me, of course, will think of you after you're gone, and think of you now, with kindness and affection. You are thought of every time I look at the leather box you made, and the holster you gave me, which are both on shelves in my living room. I also keep a photograph of you on my piano."*

I suggested the talking book program which was offered in my state. I had arranged for my mother to receive these tapes, free of charge, from the public library.

Letters from Alaska arrived less and less often. When he did write, he spoke of fatigue, who would inherit his belongings, and other end of life decisions. Still, I remembered his remarkable recovery of years past. I was busy seeing to my mother's health, as well. I kept my letters neutral and unemotional. Truth to tell, they were pretty boring.

John contracted pneumonia; said he'd recovered, but really hadn't. He didn't get out much. He was afraid of falling. He took naps. But he did find the energy to write now and then, still on his old typewriter. He sent out his "seasonal reports," (his substitute for Christmas cards) in 2001.

In January, 2002, I received his last letter. It was not even a whole page long.

"This should be short, as I don't feel much like writing—or anything else, either. That pneumonia hit me very hard, 'seems. I've not recovered from effects entirely. The talking book your mother uses probably wouldn't do me any good; my hearing being so bad— and when I'd be tired it becomes worse. Also my vision . . ." That's it, from here, at this time. All the Best, Hug, J"

Then, months of silence. I suspected the worst.

John's friend who had the antique shop in Homer had exchanged emails with me occasionally. As luck would have it, my computer died, and with it my address book containing her email address. So I wrote a note to her and sent it off snail mail. She replied,

"I'm sorry to have to tell you that John Ireland died last Saturday, April 6, at 5:30 p.m. We were with him round the clock for about the last week, and finally his systems just began to give up. His death was peaceful and he had his mind until the end. For those gifts we are thankful.

I asked him if he wanted me to notify you when he was medivaced to Anchorage and he said, 'No, what could she do?' I suggested that you might just like to know, but he insisted not. I know John set great store by your friendship. I will send you a copy of his obituary.

So ended a very special friendship. John opened windows to the wilderness for me and provided me with adventure and magnificence that I could never have experienced otherwise. For that I will always remember him and be grateful.

When the obituary arrived, I learned more about John:

John V. H. Ireland

Obituary

John Vincent Hilary Ireland was born March 12, 1914, at Hempstead, New York. His parents were Edward V. Ireland and Meta Steininger. John's mother died when he was very young, but John always spoke kindly of the substitute mothers provided for him, and proudly of his father who was an artist. His father worked for MGM Studios and was the artist for many of the theater posters for such famous movies as Gone With the Wind.

After completing two and a half years of college and working as a poultry farmer, John joined the Army at the age of 26, in 1940. He was in the Cavalry in the days when the Cavalry still actually had real horses and mules. John was sent to Saddle and Harness Maker's School by the Army and served as a Tech 5 in the Veterinary Detachment. He worked with the animals, feeding and caring for them, and as a muleskinner—the driver of a mule team pulling a wagon. After four years, his detachment was deactivated and John was discharged, receiving the American Defense Service Ribbon, the American Theater Ribbon, the World War II Victory Ribbon, the Good Conduct Medal, and Expert Rifleman Qualification.

John had difficulty settling into civilian life and he recently wrote of his move to Alaska in this manner:

Came to Alaska, Spring, 1951. Enjoyed the openness and freedom of Alaska during Territorial times.

In Alaska lived mostly in the Anchorage area. Statehood came to Alaska; again the pressure of people. Moved to a wilderness area of the Talkeetna Mountains, 50 air miles off any road. Built a cabin of dead spruce logs, using an ax to fit the corners. Lived there 21 ½ years. During that time the local wildlife watched, and when they incurred no harm from the human intrusion, they became accustomed to it and the human presence was accepted. The wilderness environment was respected, never wasted, and it seemed like the human was rewarded in always having enough . . . It was thought appropriate to write about it, by way of paying back the wilderness for its gentle care for the human, for as long as one cared to stay.

Difficulty getting a first book published. It was suggested that the book be read, accompanied by some pleasant music, and offered for sale in the form of cassette tapes. Finally the book was published, being illustrated by the author.

It seemed I was pressured from all around to return to Civilization; at age 75, the necessary survival work was becoming onerous, and I didn't seem to be learning much anymore. I had left Civilization because of not liking it, did not expect to like it upon return, and that expectation was fulfilled.

I am a "misfit:" too decrepit to live as I'd like, and discontented any other way. I'd lost my "digs" at Homer by taking a job for a year at age 79. When the job was over, I stopped at Seldovia for two years; not liking it there, I moved to Haines, at which time a serious illness affected, which was nearly the end of me; after 4 months in a hospital bed, I'm back at Homer. There may yet be some good left for me to do. (Signed, J.I.)

John was one of the last of the skilled leather crafters who used traditional hand stitching methods. The opportunity to pass this dying skill on to future generations was an important part of his later years, and last December he wrote this to a friend: *"God has been wonderful to me. Perhaps I'll be in for closer contact before long."*

So why am I now, years later, writing and remembering? As I approach the age John was when I first met him, I become more and more introspective. I wonder what kind of an influence I have had in this world. I would like to be remembered, and I would like John to be remembered. Let my words and sketches be a memorial to the unexpected, magical times that John enabled me to experience. John never asked anything of me except a listening ear and eyes that saw. Isn't that what everyone desires?

About the Author

Margery Anderson was born in Cleveland, Ohio. She taught school in Florida for 30 years and is now happily retired. Her passions are books, music, birding, and travel. She would like her epitaph to read "She lived before she died."